D0038987

# ASK ME TO DANCE

# ASK ME TO DANCE

## A Guide to Becoming More Than You Are

by

### BRUCE LARSON

A Key-Word Book
Word Books, Publisher
Waco, Texas

ASK ME TO DANCE
by Bruce Larson

First Key-Word Edition April 1978

Copyright © 1972 by Word, Incorporated
Waco, Texas 76703

Library of Congress catalog card number: 72-84396
ISBN 0-8499-4107-5
Printed in the United States of America

*To Hazel, who edited
to Mickey, who typed
and
to all those companions of The Way
who keep asking me to dance
and believe that I can*

# Contents

# Introduction

A revolution is going on in all of society and especially in the church of Jesus Christ. This book is for those people who are aware of this revolution. In the church the upheaval has very little to do with forms of government, new coalitions of denominations, music, liturgy, finely defined ethical nuances, new worship, new theological scholarship, new definitions of orthodoxy, or new spiritual athleticism. All of this is taking place, but the real revolution is much more basic and much more exciting. The people of God are asking, "How can we cooperate with him in *really* helping people? What do they need?"

The last time I was in the hospital I was shocked to discover that the routine of the hospital is built not around the needs of the patients but around the convenience of the staff. Breakfast, for instance, is often served at 5 A.M. rather than 8 A.M. This makes it possible for the outgoing staff to serve it rather than to put the burden on the busy incoming staff.

The church of Christ has often operated in the same way. We have been so busy doing religious work that we haven't been sensitive to the needs of people. Even worse, having made some kind of superficial diagnosis, we begin treatment that doesn't come anywhere near the real problem.

9

The *New York Times* printed a United Press release from Rome several years ago about a Mrs. Concetta Brigante who climbed out of a seventh-floor window of her apartment building and balanced on the ledge. The neighbors, naturally frantic, called the police. Firemen put up a ladder and forcibly rescued Mrs. Brigante. Nobody listened to her protests, and she was taken to a mental clinic as a would-be suicide.

At the clinic Mrs. Brigante finally got to tell her story. She was housecleaning and accidentally locked herself in her room. She was merely trying to get into the room next door via the ledge.

The church is full of people like Mrs. Brigante who got there by some accident. People who come in by marriage or by the invitation of a friend are suddenly caught up in some kind of program that doesn't even come near where their real hurt is.

The great Roman Catholic scholar Jacques Maritain has said, "He is always on the side of right if he is on the side of the poor." This seems like a perfectly obvious truth but the church has too rarely been on the side of those people who are simply poor—those who are broken in spirit, trying to find life and meaning and purpose within a few basic relationships. The church is geared more to harnessing people for some kind of Christian work than to helping them find the resources of God to become healthy and whole and functioning as part of a new order. We often miss knowing who the poor in spirit are. We must admit that the church does attend those who have some kind of dramatic illness. For example, there is great concern for addicts and alcoholics and the people who are going through some kind of emotional, mental, or marital trauma. But all the while people without these dramatic symptoms fill the pews, literally poor in spirit and waiting for liberation.

The church is discovering today the incredible fact that God is really *for* people. He is for people becoming all that they were meant to be and all that they yearn to become. Four marks distinguish this new church.

*1. It is learning how to speak simply.* This in itself is a profound revolution. The famous Oxford scholar, C. S. Lewis, argued that the test for ordination should require the clergy to translate difficult theological statements into common English. He says, "It is absolutely disgraceful that we expect our missionaries to the Bantus to learn Bantu, but never ask whether our missionaries to the Americans or the English can speak American or English. Any fool can write *learned* language. The vernacular is the real test. If you can't turn your faith into the vernacular, then either you don't understand it or you don't believe it."

*2. It is learning how to be real.* The church will no longer tolerate the level of life and relationships that keep people from saying it like it is and letting others know where the hurts are. R. D. Laing, in his book *Knots*, describes the illness of society which has particularly affected the church.

> They are playing a game.
> They are playing at not playing a game.
> If I show them I see they are, I shall break
>   the rules and they will punish me.
> I must play their game of not seeing that I
>   see the game.[1]

If the church is to be relevant to the needs of people, then we must talk about real hurts and real answers and be real ministers one to another.

*3. It is discovering what the priesthood of all believers is all about.* We are meant to be people who can be, in Bonhoeffer's words, "persons for others," even as Jesus was the Person for others. We are meant to be those who can cooperate with God in the liberation of our fellow beings.

One of the most creative communicators I know of today in the church is an Episcopal priest named Wes Seeliger. In a recent bulletin he wrote to his people:

Ever feel like a frog? Frogs feel slow, low, ugly, puffy, drooped, pooped. I know. One told me. The frog feeling comes when you want to be bright but feel dumb, when you want to share but are selfish, when you want to be thankful but feel resentment, when you want to be great but are small, when you want to care but are indifferent.

Yes, at one time or another each of us has found himself on a lily pad floating down the great river of life. Frightened and disgusted, we are too froggish to budge. Once upon a time there was a frog. But he really wasn't a frog. He was a prince who looked and felt like a frog. A wicked witch had cast a spell on him. Only the kiss of a beautiful maiden could save him. But since when do cute chicks kiss frogs? So there he sat, unkissed prince in frog form. But miracles happen. One day a beautiful maiden grabbed him up and gave him a big smack. Crash! Boom! Zap!! There he was, a handsome prince. And you know the rest. They lived happily ever after. So what is the task of the Church? To kiss frogs, of course.[2]

What else? A good title for this book would be "How to Kiss a Frog," for this is the heart of the revolution within the church. We have to find ways to release each other from the spell of the evil one.

*4. It is discovering a new kind of life together.* Can you envision a church in which you tell people where you hurt and expect their listening ears, their sympathy, and their prayers? Even more, a church where this is required for membership? It's inconceivable to imagine a hospital where people come in and spend years and are never asked what is wrong by the staff or even by their fellow patients. But this has happened all too often in the church. In fact, it might be rude to suggest that something is wrong. And so the church is full of people who have ceased to expect any kind of relevant help, and indeed, consider it impolite to mention pain or hurt.

This new church will be a place where illness is taken seriously and where hope for recovery and fulfillment is expected and shared. Perhaps we Christians *can* learn to kiss frogs and discover that we are surrounded by enchanted princes and princesses.

# *1*

# *Is There Life after Birth?*

Several years ago a letter came to my office addressed simply "Sir." I've found myself haunted by it. I have kept it, which is not my custom, and I read it from time to time.

After reading every issue of your magazine, I have intended to write you but I have not had the courage. Since childhood I have dedicated my life to the Christ and have done my best to serve him. But I have not known the joy nor the power that I believe a Christian should have. Furthermore, I have never met a person who had any evidence of Christian joy or power. I have never met a person whose life was changed by Christ. Very frankly, Christianity is a disappointment. I have done all I know how to do. I have tried fundamentalism, with its adherence to creeds. I have tried pietism, with its devotional emphasis. I have tried mysticism, seen a vision of Jesus bidding me come to him. I have tried liberalism, with its emphasis on social action. I have tried prayer, Bible reading, faithful church attendance, giving beyond the tithe, witnessing to others, giving to the needy. I have asked God to change my life . . . nothing ever happens. I have dared God to change my life . . . nothing ever happened. I have felt a call to the ministry, have graduated from a theological seminary, and have become an ordained minister and have done my best to faithfully serve the Christ. I am a preacher but I have nothing to preach about. I am an intercessor but I cannot pray. I am an agent of reconciliation, but I am not reconciled.

From my viewpoint God has failed. I have difficulty believing in a personal God who is concerned about people, and is able to change lives. From my point of view, the church has failed as an agent of reconciliation; the only role I see for the church is that of feeding, clothing, sheltering and counseling.

Tell me frankly; do not lie to me; can God change my life? Why has he not done so before now? Has God changed your life? How? I want a changed life. I want a ministry that amounts to something. I want my church to be a reconciling fellowship.

I guess I've kept this letter simply because the writer speaks for so many in the church. He tells what for years was my story. I was committed, I was devoted, I wanted more than anything else to be a new man in Christ and to help others become new and fulfilled. But everywhere I turned, I seemed to find sham, unreality, and religious pretense.

Just like this friend who wrote, I longed to believe that the power the Bible speaks about is true, that the breeze of the Holy Spirit can blow through lives and quicken the pulse and make people real and exciting. I too was yearning for dimensions of the life in Christ which are beyond sincerity and commitment.

The church in medieval times took this seriously. Monks talked and wrote and practiced what they called "the cure of souls." This simply meant that there was a dimension beyond conversion. When someone had a dramatic experience of Jesus Christ and joined an order to become a brother or a monk, as Martin Luther did, he was welcomed as a convert. Then he was sent to study under an older, wiser brother. This older person was a spiritual advisor who checked up on every aspect of the new convert's life. Diet, reading, conversation, devotions, and even sleeping habits came under the scrutiny of his gaze. It was believed that Jesus Christ came to make life whole and that, even as with the body, medicine for the soul must be dished out differently to each person.

The very word *salvation* comes from *salus* meaning "health" or "wholeness." The church in the Middle Ages encouraged conversion, but conversion *plus*. It practiced what we call today the medicine of the whole person.

The question is, how can we recapture this whole New Testament sense of the cure of souls which was so real in the Middle Ages? How can we help people to be more than sincere, to find more than conversion, more than doctrine? How can we help people to find life?

I believe that God has put in the hearts of all people a tremendous hunger for this kind of reality. A friend of mine, Lee Maxwell, a very creative and effective youth worker in the church, has written a poem which speaks of this hunger.

### GOD EXHALES

So here you are!
I'm found out by your presence,
I'm sorry I'm so small,
I've tried to grow
But hell . . .

There are so many games to play,
So many witticisms to say,
People to make,
But the ache . . .
Of all the crap I go through

To stay alive
Is suffocating me!

Breathe on me, breath of life,
Use your knife,
To cut away the malignancy,
To stop the spread
Of my death
With your breath.

Let's move on, out of me,
Into the world
That started my hiding from you.
Could we teach that world?
It's taught me so much.
Could we teach it?
Could we reach it?
Keep breathing, Lord.[1]

This hunger to be more than we are reminds me of a four-year-old who met an old friend of the family who had not seen the little lad for several years. "Oh, John," said the friend, "I'm surprised at how big you are!" to which the boy replied, "Oh, but I'm bigger than this!"

Our hunger to be bigger than we are could be just delusions of grandeur or it could be the very voice of God inside calling us to a larger inheritance, to a bigger stake in reality, to a truer sense of our identity as the sons of God.

This wholeness we're talking about which God wants to give is an authentic kind of life immediately recognizable to all who see it. It has very little to do with being religious, though the sincerely religious seem to be the ones who have found it in the largest degree. It's helpful to be able to isolate some of the unique marks of this wholeness. What does a cured soul look like? For me, St. Francis of Assisi embodies the essence of it. With the coming of St. Francis after the Dark Ages, a new day dawned which is still opening up. He was the light who began to shine down the long corridors of time. He fitted no preconceived categories of holy men before him. People called him God's merrymaker, the "joculator domini." G. K. Chesterton has written a magnificent book capturing something of this quality about the life of St. Francis. Here is one who was really set free by God to be himself. Because he was so free to be himself and to enjoy God, he was free to share with others and to help others to discover their gifts. He called forth a whole army of compassionate people who are still marching down the centuries as Franciscans.

Many of us who are his authentic spiritual descendants in every branch of the church reflect the very opposite of this kind of holy hilarity. Instead of brotherly love we project a kind of intense, overly serious, elder-brother paranoia. We are still doing good and preaching the Word but often without the air of liberation. We scatter gloom and heaviness rather than life and joy.

This elder-brother syndrome which has so afflicted God's people seems to have its basis in self-hate. Carl Jung, the great psychiatrist and psychologist has put it very succinctly.

Simple things are always the most difficult. In actual life it requires the greatest discipline to be simple and the acceptance of one's self is the essence of the moral problem and the epitome of a whole outlook on life. That I feed the hungry, that I forgive an insult, that I love my enemy in the name of Christ—all of these are undoubtedly virtues. What I do unto the least of these, my brethren, that I do unto Christ. But what if I should discover that the least among them all, the poorest of all the beggars, the most impudent of all the offenders, the very enemy itself—these are within me, that I myself stand in the need of the alms of my own kindness, that I am the enemy who must be loved? What then? As a rule, the Christian attitude is then reversed; there is no longer any question of love or longsuffering. We say to the brother within us, "Revenge," and condemn and rage against ourselves. We hide it from the world. We refuse to ever having met this least among the lowly in ourselves. Had it been God Himself who drew near us in this despicable form, we would have denied Him a thousand times before a single cock had crowed.[2]

Beginning to love "the enemy within" results in the style of life we see flowering in a St. Francis. He stepped into a kind of wholeness where he was reconciled to himself as well as to God and his fellow-man. That was the basis for his hilarity and freedom and for his authentic involvement and ministry. His style of life, then or now, evokes a recognition and a hunger by all.

As with the cure of the body, the cure of souls must be practiced on a one-to-one basis. Imagine, if you will, a Christian doctor who steps into his crowded waiting room and asks "Who wants to be healed?" and then proceeds to tell all who respond, "Well, the work is finished. Christ has died to make you well. Go in health and peace." The absurdity of this is obvious. He must see the patients one by one. As he works with them, he becomes a prism through which the healing power of Christ can touch each one in a different way.

Certainly healing is the work of Christ on the cross, but it must be channeled or transmitted person to person, even as in medical healing.

The New Testament reports that Jesus was called to the grave of his friend Lazarus. In the eleventh chapter of John, Mary and Martha, Lazarus's two sisters, rebuke our Lord for not coming sooner. But Jesus reminds them that all those who believe in him shall never die. At one point in this most dramatic of all Jesus' miracles, we find Jesus calling out to the dead man in the tomb, "Lazarus, come forth!" Martha, the eternal housekeeper, says, "Lord, he has been dead four days and he stinketh." In other words, "How can we handle a mess like this?" Even in her grief, her compulsion to keep life neat and orderly interferes. How much I identify with Martha since I am one who constantly counts the change in his pockets and is eternally straightening the pictures on the wall everywhere I go. Saving life is important, but for some of us, orderliness and cleanliness are even more important. Jesus came to set people like Martha and me free from such compulsions.

Lazarus, wrapped in graveclothes, hands and arms bound to his sides, hobbles out of the tomb at the command of our Lord. Jesus, by the power of God, gives life to the dead man. But the intriguing thing comes next. He turns to the friends nearby and says to them, "Loose him and let him go." You see, it is Jesus who gives life to the dead, but it is fellow Christians who are instructed to loose and unbind those who have begun to find life. We release those who have found life in Christ by our concern or we bind them by our indifference. Taking off the bandages can become the most exciting ministry of all.

This is the dimension of the church which most

excites me at present. While we are discovering that it is only God who can give life to the dead, it is only man who can unbind those who have found life. This second task is the cure of souls.

It seems to me that the church has relied almost exclusively on the mass approach of teaching and preaching in order to help people find wholeness. We have missed the fact that the ultimate cure of souls must be practiced on a person-to-person basis, taking seriously the uniqueness of each person.

I had been thinking about this whole matter for some time when my thoughts culminated one night. In a dream I saw two different men living in the same town. One man grew up as the blessed child of his parents, the envy of his brothers and sisters, the captain of his team, the president of his class, and one who walked with ease and grace among his peers. He learned early in life how to get what he wanted from people and how to use them for his own purposes. Eventually he became the head of a prospering business, with a wife of his choosing, a house full of healthy children, two cars in the garage, honors, medals, fame, and all the rest. One day he went into a little chapel and heard someone speak about a Christ who could make one a participant in the whole business of love. He heard for the first time about losing one's life for Christ, of taking up one's cross, of laying down one's life for others, of taking up a towel and a basin. He returned to his family and friends as a transformed man. Freed of the need to dominate and manipulate people, he saw that Christ could make him a servant of others. So he began to be sensitive to the needs of his wife, his children, his staff, and his friends. He entered into a whole new life of servanthood and subsequently found the joy, peace, and fulfillment that had eluded him. He became a blessing to countless people.

In time this man began to teach the adult Bible class and eventually left his business and became a preacher. He never ceased to preach about a Christ who called men to submit their lives to him and to lose their lives in service to others.

Now in this same town there was another man. The middle child of a large family, he was neglected by his mother and father. He had no sense of worth and no real identity. He never excelled in sports or academics and never held a class office. He married the first girl who'd have him, sure he'd never get a second chance. He stayed with the first company that hired him and never got very far up the organizational ladder. His life was gray and dull and meaningless until one day he happened into a little chapel and heard someone preaching about Christ as the source and center and giver of life. The gospel he heard emphasized becoming sons of God, having a crown in heaven, judging the universe, being lord of the angels, having the hairs of your head numbered, and being of infinite worth. This man began to believe he was somebody because of Jesus Christ. He came home and began to assert himself with his wife. He began to guide strongly and firmly in the lives of his children. His new quality of leadership at the office began to pay off with raises and greater responsibilities. This man, too, was asked to teach a class in his church and ultimately, because so many responded to him and to his preaching, he too entered the ministry. His gospel proclaimed that a man can do all things through Christ who lives in him. He can achieve, he can start movements and build empires.

So now we find these two born-again, spirit-filled

men attracting others. One has started a church of Dynamic Doormatism, while the other leads a church of the Holy Achievers. Each man is preaching Christ and each out of his own experience of Christ. But one is calling men to lose their lives and to serve others. The other is calling men to begin to be a somebody and to achieve great things for Christ. Each man is sincere and authentic.

But what happens to people in these two congregations? Certainly some are blessed under each man's preaching, but what happens if a nonachieving, self-hating person with no sense of worth joins the church of Dynamic Doormatism? It's no problem for him to give first place to others, since he's never been in first place. He finds that his very spiritual illness is baptized and called health.

In the church of Holy Achievers, those who are natural-born leaders and manipulators come in and find that their aggression is now baptized in the name of Christ. Once again, illness is called health.

There is no way that these two men in my dream could, simply by preaching and teaching, help all of the people who come to them. Not only will many find no help, but some will be injured. This does not minimize the value of preaching; it simply points up its limitations. Through small groups and other means, we must rediscover the priesthood of believers through which people are helped on a one-to-one basis.

I am personally convinced that this one-to-one ministry can best be practiced by amateurs. It does not require professional clergy, doctors, or psychologists, though these people can give us all tremendous insight and help. This one-to-one ministry is the authentic calling of every Christian to every other Christian

God sends his way. In my own experience, some of the people who have most dramatically helped other people are those who themselves had few external gifts. One such man was nicknamed by his congregation Frightened Freddie. Freddie was no great preacher, Freddie was no great counselor, and Freddie was no great administrator. But he believed in Christ and he believed in his people, and one by one he would listen to them and suggest the relevant next step for them. Day by day, out of his own weakness, he was (and still is) able to call forth tremendous gifts from people.

I have another friend in South Carolina who has this one-to-one relationship with her married daughter. These two beautiful women are helping each other discover what it means to be authentic Christians. One morning the mother phoned the daughter to complain at length about certain things. After listening for a long time at long-distance rates, the daughter said, "Mother, I want to be your teammate in this new adventure of life in Christ that we're both sharing. I know that's going to mean loneliness at times for both of us and I want to share your loneliness. I know at times you are going to be frightened and I want to share that with you. There's no escape from being lonely and afraid, even in the Christian life. But Mother, the things you are carrying now you don't have to carry. It's like carrying a bucket of garbage. And as your friend and prayer partner, I want you to set that bucket down and walk away from it."

"And," my friend reported, "that's exactly what I did."

You see, this is the kind of ministry that Christ calls us to. We can say the right word at the right time, we can share a burden that can't be avoided, or we can say to a friend, "Put that down and walk away from it."

Ultimately, the key to the cure of souls, as with the cure of the body, has to do with diagnosis. I believe that amateurs can practice the cure of souls if they have some simple guidelines and know what kinds of things to look for. This book is an attempt to make the reader aware of some of the components found in varying degree in every individual's life. My hope is that it will be a tool for self-diagnosis or for the diagnosis and treatment of others. The next chapters explore six of the dimensions of life germane to all of us. We will think of them as six pieces of a pie, the pie representing wholeness.

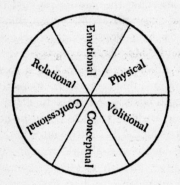

You may think of more than six; but if you check out these six things, you can make a diagnosis and begin to listen, pray, and help in a relevant way.

When we see our doctor, most of us have some presenting symptoms, for example, "I can't sleep," "I can't eat," "I'm losing weight," "I shake," and so on.

The doctor then looks for that part of the body which might be causing this and then applies surgery or medicine to that particular organ or system.

You and I are called to do the same thing with one another. We are to be aware that beyond conversion there are still things that need correcting, healing, helping, reinforcing, or adjusting. I hope that as you read these six chapters you will gain a new tool for understanding yourself and others, a new way to listen, a new way to become a friend or a counselor. In this amazing ministry of one life laid down alongside another, we need to learn how to be friends of Lazarus, how and where to begin unwrapping the bandages that bind someone whom Christ has already made alive.

## 2

# Who's in Charge?

It was during and after World War II in Germany. I had one of those rare moments of insight when I saw that all of the drama of the world, as I knew it, was being enacted in this army of occupation. Here were men who despised their present life and who were all waiting for something great to happen. Some of us were waiting to go back to wives or sweethearts. Others were waiting to go back to the farm or to a familiar and loved land. Others were waiting to go back to school or to start school to prepare for a particular kind of work. To fill the void of waiting, we did a hundred things, none of them very creative.

The tragedy seemed to be that all of us were waiting for something to begin. It struck me that hell must be a place where people are all waiting for something to begin and it never does.

During all of this, I began to notice a handful of men who seemed to be above the inertia, beyond the apathy, with a present sense of fulfillment as well as a future hope. These men were part of a small Bible study group led by our regimental chaplain, a Southern Baptist minister.

The witness of this handful of men changed me. I'll never forget kneeling down in a bombed-out apartment building in Stuttgart, Germany, where our outfit

29

was then stationed, and telling Jesus Christ that he could have my life to do with as he would. I didn't know all that was involved, but I gave him all my life, whatever that meant. That was the beginning of the adventure and I am still on it.

Perhaps because of this experience, I am convinced that the volitional plays a tremendous role in everyone's life.

Years ago in a book I don't even remember, I read what Leslie Weatherhead, the great preacher, had to say about the marks of the early church. He was contrasting the New Testament church with the church of today. He said that the early church had six things that we lack: (1) a transforming, communicable experience of the living Christ, (2) a passion to pass it on, (3) an unbreakable fellowship with the other members of the converted group, (4) a love for men which was not dependent on being loved or liked or flattered, (5) an inward serenity or peace not dependent on the number of things there are to do in a day, and (6) a deep sense of joy not dependent upon being happy.

It is interesting that the first thing on the list has to do with an experience of the living Christ that comes from some kind of decision of the will, some act of choice or commitment. Commitment itself is not the difficult thing. The difficult thing is to find something worthy of commitment. This is where Jesus speaks about himself as "The Way." He says, "The way is narrow and straight and few there are who find it." So the real choice in life is not between being committed and being uncommitted. The real choice is between being committed to the straight and narrow way which is ultimately a person or The Person or being committed to any of ten thousand kinds of goals, some high, some base.

What we ordinarily mean by the volitional is the act of commitment or surrender. However, I do not happen to like either of these words as descriptive of the great transaction. A roadsign I pass each morning on my way to work says, "Yield," which might be another term for what takes place. Yet somehow the idea of commitment or surrender or yielding seems to imply giving in to an enemy or to something that is disagreeable. These words do not convey joy, release, or the way out of a hopeless predicament.

Perhaps the idea of the contract or the covenant which is so characteristic of marriage is a better way to describe this volitional area. We joke a great deal about the shotgun marriage, in which people are forced into union. I have personally never met anyone who was really forced into marriage. People like to think they are after the marriage contract has begun. But most married people I know entered into the covenant with abandon and joy, with a sense of expectancy, and with a sense of great relief that the dismal loneliness was over and that life could now really begin.

This same joyful dimension is involved in a commitment to Jesus Christ. I suppose this call comes most clearly to those who have tried everything else and are still searching. The fact that there is Someone who calls you to life and to a life of ultimates is great good news for many. This act of volition usually has in it some of the drama of the person who has been trapped at the bottom of the hole and who sees a rope being lowered by loving and faithful hands. He commits himself to that rope, not grimly or as a sign of surrender to an enemy, but rather as to a lifeline, a savior, a hope, a way out of a predicament.

What is conversion or the act of volitionally responding to Jesus Christ? All too often conversion has been an embarrassment to the church. We seem to apologize for the fact that a person can or must make a commitment of his life to Jesus Christ. We have invented all kinds of ways to ease the pain. In a recent study Keith Miller reports that in secular psychology in Russia today the most exciting possibility is that people can be converted. If this is true, the Russian psychologists say, then life can be radically different for people in this world. In our own country men like Abraham Maslow talk about the "peak experience." They believe that people can be converted many times and that these are the great moments, or peak experiences, of life. In other words, what the church has to offer people is seen as a priceless gift by the psychologists.

William James has perhaps given us the best classical definition of conversion. In his book written in 1902, *Varieties of Religious Experience*, James defines conversion as "the process, gradual or sudden, whereby a person who is previously unhappy, inferior or wrong, becomes consciously superior, happy and right."[1] What a fantastic concept! Psychologists suggest that many secular forces can account for conversion. As Christians we believe that the supreme power in conversion is Jesus Christ himself.

Conversion is that experience that makes all the difference. It explains the incongruity of the brilliant surgeon who commits suicide because his life has become dull, while a penniless ex-alcoholic and chronic invalid finds meaning every day in a veterans hospital. One is so bored he takes his life; the other is so contagious that others find faith and help through a relationship with him.

Conversion radically alters life, giving it a new center and a new motivation. A friend and former neighbor in New Jersey is one of God's ordinary people, living a quite extraordinary life. She belongs to a church, takes care of her family, says her prayers, helps in her neighborhood. One day her mother was brutally and senselessly murdered by a young teenager for the one dollar and fifty cents which was in her purse. My friend, a middle-aged housewife, was shocked and embittered.

However, through months of praying and searching privately and with a small group of Christians that met weekly, my friend Barbara has come to the place where she has written to her mother's murderer in prison, forgiven him, visited him, and is hoping ultimately to have him paroled to her custody. Barbara's behavior is not some kind of warmed-up goodness but a newness of life which is powerful and costly. "If any man be in Christ, he is a new creation."

A New York businessman I know left his job with one of the major companies in America where he earned more than forty thousand dollars a year. He moved out to an experimental ministry in Georgia, an integrated communal farm. One dark night he was accosted by a group of local whites who smashed a bottle in his face. In spite of this, my friend feels no bitterness. He is not some starry-eyed do-gooder hurt and defeated by the rejection of those he's trying to help. The giver and source of life within him has enabled him to give up his life, materially and socially, and even to accept the rejection of those who misunderstand and hate him. He is still there, one of God's creative forces in our time.

Faith at Work has recently moved its headquarters to Columbia, Maryland, a new experimental community. A couple of friends who are taking early retirement are moving here also to share in this quality of life with us. Shortly after their decision to move, an article appeared in the *Wall Street Journal* that was not very complimentary about Columbia. This "new city," it said, has all the old problems—dope addiction among the young, crime, racial tension, divorce, suicide, and all the rest. When alarmed friends showed this article to my friend Louise, she said, "I want to move there now more than ever, for I know there will be work for me to do in helping people to find Life." To me, this demonstrates what conversion is all about. It's not a cop-out, not cotton batting to protect us from life, but a discovery of a new force, a new person, a new center in life that makes us eager to meet new challenges and to be relevant in the affairs of men.

In our ministry to people there is very little we can really do to help them unless conversion is a possibility. I have memorized a quote by Canon Quentin Warner of Canada, an Episcopal churchman now deceased who was one of God's great statesmen.

There is very little use in merely urging people to do something about their religion; all they can do is simply a projection of what they actually are. Here is a rule: If you know that a person is what he is, be neither disappointed nor irritated when he does what he does. When he has been changed to what he ought to be, he will do what he ought to have done but could not.

If people come into the Church without a transforming experience of Jesus, they will behave just as they have always behaved in the world. All the education in the world cannot make up for the fundamental need of being born again. One can become an intellectual theologian without knowing God.

That says it all. Conversion is not just one way to live but the only way out of a life of inefficiency, ineffectiveness, irrelevancy, and hopelessness. It is God's good gift to us in Jesus Christ.

How does one go about being converted? How does one give his life to Christ? First, I think we must understand that this act of commitment or this act of the will is not a commitment to support an idea, even though that idea is biblically sound. Neither is it to an ethic, that is, to a promise to be pure, good, noble, chaste, sober for the rest of your life. It's not basically a commitment to support the Bible or biblical truth, nor even a commitment to support the church. Rather, commitment is a call to be the church. It is literally the same as when one says to another, "Will you marry me?" The response is not true or false but yes or no. This is the real dynamic of Christian conversion. The Bible speaks about having the mind of Christ. You invite another person to live inside of you when you yield a part of yourself to him and make room for him at the center. This Person then has a plan for your life and begins to supply new direction, new resources, new strengths.

Some of the saddest people I know are those who have set about to build the Kingdom of God without ever having been converted. In time the human juices and vision run out and there is no resource there to replenish. And surely there is no sadness in the world like that experienced by the man who abandons the goals and principles he once loved and served and thought secure and permanent. Dorothy Parker sums this up for us in her poem to middle-age, entitled "The Veteran."

> When I was young and bold and strong,
> Oh, right was right and wrong was wrong,
> My plume on high, my flag unfurled,
> I rode away to fight the world.
> "Come out you dogs, and fight!" said I
> And wept, there was but once to die.
>
> But I am old and good and bad
> Are woven in a crazy plaid,
> I sit and say, "The world is so
> And he is wise who lets it go.
> A battle lost, a battle won,
> The difference is small, my son."
>
> Inertia rides and riddles me!
> The which is called philosophy.[2]

And so, since this act of the will is not to ideals, but to a Person, it is usually more meaningful to have a witness present. We have a witness present at the marriage ceremony although it's not a must and certainly a common-law marriage is a possibility. We are so constructed that when a third party can hear us turning over the reins of our life to The Person, there is something binding and cosmic about that. My own initial commitment was not made in the presence of another, but soon after I did have a witness to my new allegiance and have had many witnesses since.

It has been said that this act of the will is initially wholesale, and then every day retail, as the price for that day becomes clear. That is to say, it has a beginning and it is a process. There is a particular price in the beginning and there is a continuing and changing price in the process. Again, as in marriage, one seldom knows what the marriage will cost six months or a year or ten years after the ceremony. The bridegroom and the bride may be aware of the immediate cost involving money, lack of freedom, and accountability to each other, but as that initial pledge is renewed daily the cost and the joy are constantly changing and growing. The discipline at the heart of all Christian commitment is just as implicit or explicit as the discipline required for all successful marriages.

In the first church that I served after I was ordained to the ministry, a number of us had been converted and were beginning to live out this new life in Christ. We soon discovered our need to affirm our commitment daily, and so together we drew up a covenant that we kept for many years. I suspect some of us are still keeping it, even though most of us have since moved to many parts of the nation and the world. Here is the covenant which seemed to speak to our need at that time.

1. To keep a one-half hour of devotion at a set time daily.
2. To pray continually throughout the day, offering up flash prayers for self or others, or situations, and to give thanks.
3. To share life in a small group.
4. To make retreat personally two hours monthly. (This means two hours alone with God for inventory, confession, intercession, thanksgiving, future plans, rereading of marriage vows, ordination vows, etc.)
5. To express my Christian vocation in specific social action (such as: care for or service to needy, sick, orphans, shut-ins, handicapped;

community betterment; or political, interracial or intercultural programs, etc.).

6. To tithe consistently.
7. To offer grace at each meal. (This should be done quietly and without ostentation in public, we decided.)
8. To share worship daily with my household, weekly in church.
9. To live frugally, practicing simplicity in my spending, eating, keeping fit, sleeping enough, using my surplus for others. (We decided that living frugally would be defined to mean "the judicious use of all of our resources, including time, talents, money, health.")
10. To grow intellectually as a Christian, reading a solid book at least monthly.

This covenant is almost twenty years old. But such covenants, as with marriage vows, are timeless. The books one reads or the way one prays or worships may change as we grow, but the idea of a covenant community together is a constant.

Commitment is the solution to the universal problem of identity. Life keeps asking, "Who are you?" and I keep asking myself, "Who am I?" I am who I belong to. So many people today belong to the company they serve which demands their time and allegiance. A man I know was let go as the president of his company because of a merger with a larger company. Money was no problem as he had a substantial bank account, but his life fell apart because he didn't know who he was apart from being a company president. His uncertainty eventually led him into a commitment of his life to Jesus Christ.

Even Dietrich Bonhoeffer, the great Christian leader

and anti-Nazi spokesman, began to wonder who he was while confined in a German prison. His struggle is revealed in his classic poem, "Who Am I?"

Who am I? They often tell me
I step from my cell's confinement
calmly, cheerfully, firmly,
like a squire from his country-house.
Who am I? They often tell me
I talk to my warders
freely and friendly and clearly,
as though it were mine to command.
Who am I? They also tell me
I bear the days of misfortune
equably, smilingly, proudly,
like one accustomed to win.

Am I then really all that which other men tell of?
Or am I only what I know of myself,
restless and longing and sick, like a bird in a cage,
struggling for breath, as though hands were compressing my throat,
yearning for colours, for flowers, for the voices of birds,
thirsting for words of kindness, for neighbourliness,
tossing in expectation of great events,
powerlessly trembling for friends at an infinite distance,
weary and empty at praying, at thinking, at making,
faint, and ready to say farewell to it all?

Who am I? This or the other?
Am I one person today, and tomorrow another?
Am I both at once? A hypocrite before others,
and before myself a contemptibly woebegone weakling?
Or is something within me still like a beaten army,
fleeing in disorder from victory already achieved?
Who am I? They mock me, these lonely questions of mine.
Whoever I am, thou knowest, O God, I am thine![3]

If you believe as I do that commitment to Jesus Christ is the answer to this identity problem, then how do we help people make that kind of commitment?

First of all, any Christian who wants to be instrumental for another in meeting Christ can be used in this way. A friend of mine, an elder in a very large Southern Presbyterian church, had for years wanted the ability to introduce other people to Jesus Christ. When he expressed this wish on a session retreat with the other elders, a brother prayed for him and asked God to give him this gift. He shared with me, with real excitement, that since that time he has been able to lead dozens of people to Jesus Christ, including some other elders! Introducing people to Christ and helping them to find conversion is not a technique or a gimmick. It means being used by God in the way he wants to use us when we are willing.

However, it is important to remember not to push people. It was thrilling to hear Dr. Paul Tournier, the eminent Swiss psychiatrist and author of so many exciting books about personal counseling, tell some of us the secret of his own ministry. He felt people had misunderstood Jesus when he talked about being fishers of men. "After all," he said, "no one wants to be caught by somebody else. So I sit by the bank without a fishing pole in my hand and enjoy the scenery. Fish seem to sense that I'm not trying to catch them. They come to me just to talk about themselves and about life. Then from time to time, some do get caught by Jesus Christ and I am more surprised than they are."

It is essential, too, to be available to people when they are ready and not when we are ready. There is a tremendous hunger in people to find this new life in Christ and if we are available at their times of peak need, we can be "a person for others."

Finally, when a person is seeking, don't try to sell him your brand of theology or ethics or the doctrines of your church. Simply say in some form, "Well, if you want to meet Christ, he's here and he loves you. He died for you, he wants to live in you. If you're tired of running your own life and you want him to take over, tell him and I will be your witness."

Is this volitional dimension really that easy? Yes and no. Even for the converted, those who have made this great transaction, doubts and fears come. Kaj Munk, a Danish minister who was executed by the Nazis for aiding the Jews, wrote this just before he died.

Yes, perhaps it is all a mistake, this business about Christianity. Sometimes it really looks to me like that. Perhaps all this talk about God and Jesus Christ and the salvation of men is just a collection of fairy tales. And I am a minister. Perhaps this is a mistake too. Perhaps a mistake to preach love and forgiveness in a hate-torn world, to rescue those who are in need, to teach the children, to comfort the lonely and the dying. But if it is, after all, a mistake, then it is a beautiful mistake. If Christianity should turn out, after all, to be true, then unbelief will have been a very ugly mistake.

And so it is for those with a new center in their life. We stand with Kaj Munk or perhaps with Martin Luther and say, "Here I stand. God help me, I can do no other." Like a bridegroom separated from his loved one, we know by faith that we belong and that we are possessed and that we are loved. This is what faith is all about.

# As a Man Thinketh

In an historic church in Springfield, Illinois, the rumor went out that a certain lawyer had experienced a remarkable conversion. Apparently, it had affected his marriage, his relationship to his children, and his job. I met this man at a retreat hosted by his church and was assigned to stay in his home. The first night, as we sat in his study to talk, I asked my new friend how the change in his life had come about. Without hesitation, he replied, "It happened when I read *The Shaking of the Foundations* by Paul Tillich."

I was amazed. "I never met anybody who got converted reading Tillich," I said.

"Well, I did. For years I was confused about life—its purpose, its direction, meaning. It all made me very depressed. Reading Tillich, I began to see that there is order in the universe, purpose, direction. Jesus Christ spoke to me through that book."

Since then, I have been convinced that there are a great many people who come into the Christian life through the dimension of the conceptual, people who need to see something of the landscape of reality before they can be gripped by God. Perhaps this was not the way I came in because basically I am not a theologian or a scholar. For me, Truth is much more existential, and I tend to live in a more relational dimension. But I am aware that there are people who need one glimpse of truth, one sidelong glance at God's blueprint, in order to respond to his love and purpose in Jesus Christ.

The Bible speaks repeatedly of this need for the conceptual. It abounds in dynamic truths like "Without a vision, the people perish." In America we have seen how on the national scene a man can bring a vision of dedication and service to a whole people that unites and, for a time at least, brings healing to the land.

For years we have seen the effects of a negative vision in the Communist world. People have been brainwashed and given a totally different understanding of the landscape of reality. Ultimate power does not rest with missiles, armies, and parliaments. Ultimate power is the ability to alter a man's mind or the mind of a people and forcibly inject a whole new set of values.

The conceptual dimension has the power to transform life negatively or positively. Through a great picture, through a sermon, through a book by Paul Tillich, or through a course taught by an inspired professor we can suddenly move from the false and unreal world to a landscape of reality which is endless and boundless, painful and terrifying.

Years ago a friend brought me a small picture of Grunewald's "Crucifixion," and it hangs in my private study at home. If you have ever seen this picture, you know the stark horror it creates, a far cry from the usual painless-looking crucifixion. It is one man's attempt to show something of the agony of God's suffering in Jesus Christ as he identified with and died for this world.

There is a story about this picture being hung in a

mental hospital many years ago. Supposedly, many patients came to emotional and mental health by living with this picture and coming to grips with the idea that they are loved at a terrible cost by God in Jesus Christ.

In my first church a very dear friend who was an artist actually had a conversion of sorts when he discovered Rembrandt's head of Christ. Here is an attempt by one of the great artists to show the humanity of Christ and at the same time his divinity. Having grown up with all of the Sunday school pictures of Christ, my friend was gripped by the wonder and the splendor of the incarnation as it is captured by one artist.

What is the power of the conceptual? To understand it, we need to study not only those who have been captured by the Christian concept, the great vision, but some of the motivating concepts of the secular movements as well.

The success of the Communist ideology is certainly one of the strongest examples of the power of the conceptual, especially in its early years. In his book *Witness* Whittaker Chambers describes vividly how this works.

The vision inspires. The crisis impels. The working man is chiefly moved by the crisis. The educated man is chiefly moved by the vision. The working man, living upon a mean margin of life, can afford few visions. An educated man, peering from the heart of the Harvard Yard, or any college campus, upon a world in chaos, finds in the vision the two certainties for which the mind of man tirelessly seeks: a reason to live and a reason to die. No other faith of our time presents them with the same practical intensity. That is why Communism is the central experience of the first half of the 20th century, and may be its final experience, unless the free world in the agony of its struggle with Communism overcomes its crisis by discovering, in suffering and pain, a faith which will provide man's mind, at the same intensity, with the same two certainties: a reason to live and a reason to die.[1]

Although that statement was written about twenty years ago, it is prophetic of the time into which we are moving and the emergence of a new kind of church in our time. Though it was dim, Whittaker Chambers had a vision for a possible revival of faith that could capture the minds of a significant number of people in the last half of the twentieth century.

In describing the vision, he talks about two certainties it must supply, a reason for living and a reason for dying. Let me add two more to this. An adequate conceptual view of life should also supply people with an explanation of evil and some strategy for the promotion of righteousness, both personally and corporately. It seems to me that man is becoming disillusioned not only with his reasons for living and dying but with his understanding of evil and what to do about it. He needs to learn how to take arms against a sea of trouble and bring some kind of wholesome solution.

One of the most fascinating men of the twentieth century was the English scholar and Christian apologist C. S. Lewis. Perhaps of all Christian writers he has helped me most to understand sin and evil and the strategy for righteousness. Lewis has been called by his peers and fellow scholars one of the most powerful and best trained intellects in the world. Certainly his own conversion was in the area of the conceptual as much as the volitional. He was thirty-one years old and had served in the British army in World War I, studied at Oxford, and returned there to teach. Lewis had always considered himself a devout atheist. During his early days at Oxford, when his atheism was in full bloom, he found he had to keep his guard up, else God would close in on him. "A young atheist cannot guard his faith too carefully," he once said.

The real turning point in Lewis's life came when the Ultimate Reality who is Jesus Christ did close in upon him. Lewis describes himself as the most reluctant convert in all England, being dragged into the Kingdom by his heels, kicking and screaming. As he came in, this brilliant mind was suddenly gripped by truth. Few people have helped me, as well as countless thousands of others, to discover more of the landscape of reality than this explorer. He wrote a number of books that describe simply what faith is and how it works in every dimension. But I think his greatest contributions are in the area of the novel. He wrote two series of novels; one series, the Narnia novels, are really fairy stories for small children. But, like other great children's stories such as *Winnie the Pooh* and *Wind in the Willows,* they are really too advanced for children to understand and appreciate. However, Lewis felt that great teaching could be absorbed through myth and legend, through concept and illusion. In the Narnia stories he deals with evil and the forms it takes. He deals with God, Jesus, and the poor struggling creatures who try to be obedient and who fail.

In his second set of novels, of which there are three, he moves into the realm of science fiction and writes explicitly for adults. He talks about life on other planets and the whole cosmic nature of good and evil. He deals with the implications for the whole universe in the fact that God became man on one little pea-sized planet. His writing ministry, I suppose, has helped countless people to obtain an adequate vision or an adequate grasp of truth that resulted in their being dragged into the Kingdom like Lewis. Others have flung their lives into the Kingdom, hoping to meet that Ultimate Being about whom Lewis writes so lucidly.

One of my favorite heroes in secular literature is Cervantes's wonderful character of Don Quixote, recently popularized by the musical *Man of La Mancha*. Don Quixote was a crazy old man captured by the concept of the struggle in the world between good and evil and the need for men of virtue like himself to get into the arena of life and fight oppressors and evildoers. We all know of his struggles against the windmills that he thought were giants and of his disastrous encounter with sheep and peasants.

The beauty of Don Quixote's story, however, is in what happens to him as his vision motivates him and spreads a powerful contagion to others. Because of his concepts, he changes and others change for the better. The Bible captures this timeless, powerful truth of which Quixote is an example with the words, "As a man thinketh, so is he."

This kind of vision is not limited to fictional characters. I have known men so grasped by an idea that they literally flung their lives into some adventure which lead to the liberation of scores of people. One of them is Bill Stringfellow. Bill, though a very controversial fellow in most circles, is one of the great theological minds in America. In the early years of his life, he was transformed by Christ through reading the Bible. Graduated at the top of his class from law school, he moved into Harlem, that part of America where the ratio of lawyers to the general population is the lowest. He lived there in a cold-water, sixth-floor, unheated tenement for many years, identifying with people and helping them spiritually as well as legally. Bear in mind that no dramatic conversion and no particular individual was responsible for Bill's initial change. The power of the Ultimate Concept, that of God in Jesus Christ speaking through the Bible, motivated Bill to become truly a Don Quixote of our time. Identifying with the black and the poor and the oppressed, he leads a whole army of those who have been inspired by his writings and by his example.

The power of a vision is not always communicated by words. Stringfellow got a concept of the Christ through reading the Bible. Many others saw Christ through Stringfellow's example as he lived out his life during those dark and difficult years in Harlem. In other areas of life as well we find the conceptual is communicated by models as well as by words. Listen to Whittaker Chambers again from his book *Witness*.

One day in the great jury room of the Grand Jury of the Southern District of New York, a juror leaned forward slightly and asked me, "Mr. Chambers, what does it mean to be a Communist?" I said, "When I was a Communist, I had three heroes."

Felix Djerjinsky was a Pole Ascetic, highly sensitive, intelligent and a Communist. As a young man and a political prisoner in Warsaw, he insisted on being given the task of cleaning the latrines of the other prisoners. For he held that the most developed member of any community must take upon himself the lowliest tasks as an example to those who are less developed.

Eugene Levine was a German Jew and also a Communist. When the Bavarian Soviet Republic was crushed, the court martial told him, "You are under sentence of death." Levine answered, "We Communists are always under sentence of death."

The third man was Sazonov, a Russian. When imprisoned at a terrible prison camp in Siberia, he sought to protest the flogging of the other men. He finally drenched himself in kerosene, set himself on fire and burned himself to death.[2]

Here we see the incarnation principle at work in the secular world. The power of the concept when it is incarnate in another's life is even more irresistible than when it is embodied in Rembrandt's head of Christ or Grunewald's "Crucifixion." What motivated Whittaker Chambers to become one of the most dedicated Communists of his time was something beyond the principles of the Communist party. It was the dedication he saw in the lives of several men who were committed to those principles. Eventually, of course, Chambers went beyond the witness of men to find Jesus Christ himself.

Let me mention four situations in which I know the power of the conceptual to transform life is taken very seriously. These four places, however, do not rely solely on the conceptual to change and motivate men. They would also affirm the need for the first dimension, the volitional.

The Church of The Saviour in Washington, D.C., is a tiny covenant band of people who have made a mark, not only upon Washington but upon church life across our land and around the world. At the heart of this unique fellowship is the idea that people need more than conversion. There must be some intensive training for people's minds to be reoriented around the truths that God has begun to reveal in Jesus Christ. To become a member of The Church of The Saviour, therefore, one must successfully complete two years of courses in the Bible, Christian ethics, and theology.

The second group is Kittamaqundi Community, an experimental church in my town, the new city of Columbia, Maryland, that is an offshoot of The Church of The Saviour. This is a group that is developing the same style of life which relies heavily on conversion and then emphasizes the teaching ministry. Here, as in The Church of The Saviour, one must successfully complete basic courses over a two-year period before membership in the community becomes an option.

The Ecumenical Institute in Chicago is a third force in our time that takes seriously the power of the conceptual. With ministries all around the country, this group believes that society can be changed and that new leadership must be trained. They stress the necessity for new concepts and new ideas, considering why the old is failing and where the new must begin.

A fourth example of a movement within the evangelical part of the church which leans heavily on the conceptual is L'Abri Fellowship in Switzerland. Francis Schaeffer, author of many books, is its leader.

The conceptual dimension is certainly important, but there is more to the Christian life than disembodied truths and concepts. There is a life, and it is a person called Jesus Christ who calls us into relationship with him. As we respond to him, we are led by this incarnate and indwelling Lord into the most fantastic realms of concepts. Paul says, "Let this mind be in you which was in Christ Jesus." Through this mind of Christ we begin to see the universe in a new way, to study the actions and interactions of men from a different perspective.

As Christians we must begin to take seriously the conceptual struggles of men, whether they are learned deans in great universities or bearded bards in blue jeans.

# 4

# What about Guilt?

I pulled up to a gas station once in the heart of Newark, New Jersey, to ask directions. I was looking for a meeting of young people where I was to lead a workshop. I bought some gas, and as I gave the attendant my credit card, I said, "I'm lost." Noticing that my credit card was marked "Reverend," he smilingly said, "Ah, I see you're a clergyman. So you're not really lost like most of us."

"Oh, but I am," I replied. "Being a clergyman doesn't mean that you can't be lost in some of the most basic areas of life. It just means that you ought to know where to go for help." The man shook his head; he would not and could not believe that a clergyman could be as lost as he was.

This is a parable of people in the church. We might be lost, but we can't believe that a fellow Christian or fellow church member or fellow deacon or elder or fellow women's association officer could be like us, and so we live as part of a conspiracy of silence and we die for the lack of real communication and the help that God can give through it. The power of confession, the third piece of our pie of wholeness, is essential to our Christian life.

It's interesting to trace the history of confession in the Christian church. The church, of course, officially began at Pentecost after our Lord's death and resurrection, with the coming of the Spirit. But the foundation for the church as we know it was laid by our Lord's own life and ministry and his relationships with his disciples and the people of Palestine. During his three years of ministry Jesus must have been a very open person. How else could we know about his temptation in the wilderness? No other human being was there. How would we know about his discouragements, his sorrows, his fear of the cross, his agony before God as he wrestled with the Father's will? We know about them only because our Lord himself disclosed them to faithful men who passed them on to us.

After the church was born at Pentecost, we find a little society meeting in homes, basements, caves, catacombs, and quickly multiplying all over the inhabited world. For the first four hundred years we know through historical record that Christians practiced confession in the fellowship. When someone committed a sin, it was shared openly in the entire worshiping congregation.

Then as the church grew, it became both embarrassing and difficult for everyone to be honest with everyone else in his particular congregation of believers, his branch of the company of the committed. So with the emergence of persons designated as clergy, and with the growth of the church, the method of confession became optional. A believer had the choice of confessing to a clergyman or priest, or in the fellowship of the church. But by the thirteenth century, as worship became more formal, we find that confession was sealed off and was from then on heard only by a priest. Sometime later the Protestant Reformers, trying to discover the roots of authentic Christian life and to recapture the power of the early church, talked about the priesthood of all believers. This was largely interpreted to mean not that every Christian was a priest to his brother, but that no Christian needed a priest because we had Christ. Confession to a brother was a rarity.

From that time until the present, the power of the church has tended to diminish as confession became less public and more private. Simultaneously mental and emotional illness has grown and, in point of fact, taken such a giant step that psychosis is one of the primary illnesses of our time. I cannot help but see a connection between the growth of mental illness and the sealing off of the confessional.

Today no one doubts the need for confession. All of us live with a tremendous amount of guilt. I suppose it's always been true, but, in these times especially, we are faced with many everyday choices that leave us with guilt. Picture a man who has promised his wife that he will spend the evening with her since for many nights he has been away on all kinds of civic and church work. Just as he is leaving his office, he meets a friend in great need of a listening ear. He then has to decide whether he will renege on his promise to his wife or leave a brother in possibly serious trouble. I am suggesting that there is no way out of that dilemma without feeling real guilt. To live outside of a monastery entails living with real guilt. Or, perhaps life in a monastery is even more guilt-producing because it is so uninvolved with the hurts and needs of the real world. The Christian does not leave his guilt behind him. A guided life does not produce a guiltless life. Learning how to deal with guilt is the heart of the matter.

Helping people to deal with their guilt is part of our ministry as Christians and involves this confessional dimension of life. In the Lazarus story Jesus gives his followers the power to unbind others. He tells us elsewhere that we have the keys to the Kingdom, and those whom we let in are let in and those whom we keep out are kept out. In the Book of Acts, when the risen Lord confronts the Apostle Paul (at that time called Saul) on the road to Damascus, Paul's life is not immediately changed. Rather, he is led into Damascus, miserable, his life tumbled in, sick, blind, and unable to eat. Three days later a layman named Ananias walks in, sent there because of his dialogue with God during his morning quiet time. It's at the hands of Ananias that the power of the Holy Spirit falls upon Paul. His sight and his health are restored, and he becomes a new being in Christ.

And what happened between Paul and Ananias? Certainly Paul was able to open up his heart to a brother and talk about the Christians he had killed as a result of his well-meaning zeal. He probably also talked about other mistakes in his life. Ananias was not only Paul's confessor, but he could pronounce absolution in the name of Jesus. He could pray with Paul and see God's healing come.

Several years ago I received a letter which was sent to two other men as well. In part this is what it said.

Dear Bruce and Frank and Jack,

I am sending a copy of this letter by way of greeting to all three of you. You have all meant so much to me and I have procrastinated too long in telling you what has happened. [There follows a description of his wife's emotional and mental illness and how he finally got in touch with the doctor she was seeing, a clinical psychologist.] The doctor's theory is based on openness and the ability to admit to the significant others in our lives the exact nature of our wrongs. I was John Smith, though. I had been to three Christian conferences and I had committed my life to Christ, admitting one thing that had been wrong.

Beyond that, I couldn't have any wrongs because I had been saved. I got to talk to this doctor after lunch and I found out some of my wrongs. [He then lists several sins he shared with the doctor.] Then the doctor asked about money. I said, "Yes, I had taken ten or fifteen cents out of our cash register at dad's store a lot of different times." The doctor then asked about now, and I said, "Oh, nothing." Then I started to think. It was pretty easy to forget to ring up some of the checks that came in and have the extra money around to make me look like a big shot, and then it just got to be a habit and so much was channeled out monthly. The doctor then asked if there was anything else and I said I didn't think so. He then wanted to know if I was willing to go in and tell the group therapy people these things. I said yes and I did. The group gave me strength, certainly not in approving of what I'd done but of helping me bear the burden. They asked if my wife knew of this and I said no, and I didn't think so. And I went to my wife and told her all.

A couple of weeks later I found myself back in the group, telling my story again. One of the people in the group mentioned something about restitution. I wasn't taking money anymore, but paying it back had never occurred to me. My wife helped me to see that I had to tell the authorities. So I went to my C.P.A. and told him my story and how much had been withheld. What it amounted to was that I owed money plus interest to the Internal Revenue Service for income tax. The C.P.A. went back and refigured the tax returns for the eight years involved, and we made a voluntary disclosure to the Internal Revenue Service. It cost me close to one thousand dollars in interest for my stupidity. I was then able to go to the significant others in my life and tell my wrongs . . . [Further on in the letter, as he is about to close:] Once I had cleaned my skirts, I was in a better position to help my wife. She seems to have made more improvement lately.

It seems to me that my friend's psychiatrist played a role not unlike that of Ananias in his encounter with Paul. But my Christian brother did not find this basic kind of help in his church or in the conferences he attended. It was at the hands of a secular psychologist in a secular group that God was able to bring in the dimension of the confessional and bring about restitution which has made him a whole and free person. In the church we are seldom able to tell others where we have failed, let alone be encouraged to make restitution.

I feel great admiration for the Roman Catholic church which for two thousand years has clung tenaciously to this dimension of the confessional as a part of the cure of souls and of helping people to become new. And they have made this available for all of their members.

Those of us in the Reformed tradition had to wait for Freud and psychoanalysis to discover man's need for the confessional ingredient in wholeness. We are in debt to these apparently incongruous streams—the Roman Catholic church and psychoanalysis. For, while each mistrusted the other, they have kept alive this source of healing to sick people.

I mentioned earlier that the volitional dimension was the turning point in my life and indeed it was. When I gave my life to Christ, my direction changed. Then conceptually, I began to study more, to be caught up in doctrine and theology. But for years after my conversion. I found that I was still ineffective. I was unable to love myself, to love others, to relate.

I was justifying myself. And all this behind the façade of being a Christian.

The real turning point came at a meeting in New York where people of all denominations and colors and creeds and conditions were learning how to be open and honest with one another, or, as they called it, "to walk in the light." It was in this crowd that I discovered the difference between forgiveness and cleansing. I had claimed the forgiveness of Christ on the cross years before, over in Germany after World War II. I knew that I was forgiven and that I lived as a man who was forgiven. But the Bible speaks about confessing your sins one to another so that you might be healed. It goes on to say that if we confess our sins he is faithful and just to forgive us our sins and to *cleanse* us from all unrighteousness. As I opened my life to another friend, I found the power of God and the cleansing of God, even as Paul must have found it on Straight Street in conversation with Ananias.

The Gospels are full of this power that God releases through the confessional. Look what happened to Zaccheus when Jesus, passing through town, came to have dinner with him. We can see the two men probably alone in Zaccheus's dining room. Suddenly, Zaccheus opens his heart and begins to tell Jesus how he got his money and how he used people, and eventually he promises to make amends. At the end of their meal Zaccheus has found such newness of life that Jesus says, "Today salvation has come to your house."

I have often heard Paul Tournier, the Swiss physician and counselor, say that the turning point for him was not his conversion. For years he was a Bible-believing, church-going, converted Christian, but without effectiveness or power. Then one day in New York he went to a small meeting in a home where people were simply being themselves, sharing deeply of hurts, joys, sins, excesses. It was in this climate that Tournier became new, and when he returned to Geneva and his medical practice, he suddenly found people opening up to him. Instead of talking only about their physical symptoms, patients began to talk about their lives. The dimension of the confessional turned Tournier into the amazing counselor he is today. Founder of the society of medicine to the whole person, he is practicing the cure of souls with amazing results.

I believe everyone needs a confessor because our basic sin is pride. That which keeps us from being in a real and open relationship with God and one another is usually not our sin but our pride in not revealing our sins. As Christians we believe that Christ died for our sins, but if I cannot tell my brother about my sin which has been forgiven, that makes me unreal and phony with him. The Bible speaks much about this and about the fact that our real sin is self-justification.

Take, for example, two men in the Bible who demonstrate two radically different ways to handle sin. One is King David and the other is Moses' brother Aaron. One is a liberator of men and the other is a roadblock to God's purposes. One man is full of joy and abandon and grace; the other man is reluctant, dragging his feet, full of questions and regrets. Now, the difference between these two men is not in their goodness, for both have sinned. It is not even in the degree of sin, though David is by human standards, I suppose, a greater sinner than Aaron. David is an adulterer, a thief, a liar, and a murderer. But these two men deal with their guilt very differently. When David is nailed again and again by God through people or circumstances, he is quick to admit to God and to his fellowmen that he has sinned, to make restitution, and to believe that he is loved by a God who will and does forgive.

Aaron, on the other hand, denies his guilt. When Moses comes down from the mountain, having talked with God, and sees the people dancing before a golden calf instead of worshiping God, he rightly blames Aaron. But Aaron says, "I don't know what happened. We didn't make any calf. We simply threw all of our gold utensils and jewelry into the fire and out came this calf." Aaron had to justify himself and so missed God's forgiveness while David lived in the dimension of the confessional and therefore could experience grace.

Because the Reformed part of the church has been so unwilling to take the confessional dimension seriously, we find psychology taking the lead. The new psychology, which is really a revolt against some of the Freudian emphasis, treats emotional disturbance by helping people to accept responsibility, or blame, for their problems. Under the Freudian system, responsibility for failure was placed on parents, friends, wife or husband, all those who allegedly treated the patient badly. The new psychology views the individual himself as the one who is basically hiding his guilt and refusing to take the blame. These new psychologists consider the neurotic and even the psychotic a person who has a fairly well-developed superego that is not quite strong enough to keep him from yielding to temptation. After he succumbs, the individual's conscience begins to bother him. The patient starts hiding his deviant acts from others, and, in order to hide, he must lie. And in order to cover up one lie, he has to tell more lies. So the first step in this chain of illness leads to a neurosis and to the kind of behavior which leaves him socially vulnerable. He becomes more and more secretive, seclusive and cut off from all the world around him.

The new psychologists believe that this self-inflicted secrecy encourages illness and prevents healing. The patient is afraid that someone is going to find out about him, so he continually leads a guarded life, one marked by anxiety and the dread of exposure. The more he hides and conceals, the less he is able to share intimately with others and the less he dares to have any meaningful contact with other people. He tends to become an authority in subjects so that he can speak, preach, teach, or lead and thereby avoid any kind of intimate relationship. Ultimately, he deliberately avoids any attempt to relate, even to members of his family, his peer group, or his community because relating to others has become so threatening. He becomes a closed person.

Men like Hobart Mowrer, who have been leading in this new psychology, believe that there are only two paths available to such a closed, alienated person. He can reveal his real self and become an open person, or he can start believing his own lies and begin more completely to inhabit his unreal world. The second alternative usually leads the neurotic into the typical syndromes of schizophrenia. The world of delusions and hallucinations becomes the real world, and the world of reality becomes unreal.

The church needs to discover what some of these psychologists are discovering and what Roman Catholics have kept alive for centuries. We can be confessors one to another and thereby tap a dimension of God's Holy Spirit that can bring healing to all those who are willing to know and be known.

How do we go about hearing a confession as a Christian to a Christian? First, care about the person whom God has placed next to you in some situation. Next, it may seem right to share something of your own particular needs of the moment and to begin to make him your confessor. Third, listen to your friend. Let him know that you are eager to listen and that you count it a privilege. I call this aggressive listening. People want to be listened to and if they find a genuine, aggressive listener, most people will open up at increasingly deep levels. Fourth, ask some basic questions, for example: How are your relationships on the job? How are you and your wife getting on? Are you able to relate to your kids? These are not judgmental questions. They merely let the other person know that you are concerned about how the deep things of his life are coming along.

In no sense am I saying that one should pry out of somebody else his secrets. Actually, this is impossible. No one can pry anyone's secrets out of him. Sidney Jourard says in *The Transparent Self:*

Man's self, as near as now known, can never be known to any save the experiencing individual, unless the individual man unequivocally cooperates and makes his self known. In short, man must consent; if we would know his self, he must want to tell us. If he doesn't wish to tell us of his self, we can torture him, browbeat him, tempt him, even make incisive psychoanalytic guesses; but unless he wishes to make his self known, we will, of course, never know.[1]

But the new church is not only a society of those who hear *formal* confessions one to another, which is always a continuing thing, but a society of those who "walk in the light." Walking in the light means living without secrets. Your motives, your attitudes, your decisions are shared quite informally through the course of the week in the many situations in which you find yourself with other Christians. To be a part of a small group of people who live this way can be one of the most challenging and liberating experience that I know.

Pope John XXIII brought this dimension to the entire Christian world. He was a walking confession, a real man who was also a Christian, who was also the pope. After being elected pope, one of his first acts of office was to visit one of the large jails in Rome. As he was there giving the prisoners his blessing, he told the men that the last time he had been in jail was to visit his brother. What a breath of fresh air! The pope, considered Christ's vicar on earth, came from a real family and knew what it was to share the hurts and joys of all men everywhere.

The meaning of the phrase *walking in the light* came to me many years ago on a Pennsylvania highway near Scranton in the middle of the night. As I was driving along, I took the wrapper off some candy and, finding the ashtrays in the car full, I opened the window and threw it out. Suddenly I realized that I would never have done this in the daylight. Somehow, the very darkness encouraged me to litter, a thing I deplore. Daylight, on the other hand, reminds us of our responsibility to other people and helps us to do the responsible thing.

People who do not live in fellowship with others live in perpetual darkness and continually do things of which they are ashamed. But people who live in a fellowship where they know and are known live in the light and are encouraged to be and to do those things of which they can be proud.

Most of us see the need to confess those acts that are blatantly wrong, but what about those things that are just a little dishonest and that can begin to erode our very integrity and personality? I am still embarrassed to remember an experience years ago involving a luggage rack for our car. When our children were all small, we traveled with an amazing array of cribs, carriages, mattresses, and diapers. One station wagon was not enough to handle five Larsons and baggage.

So, I bought a luggage rack to use on our vacation and it was terrible! It kept slipping off and simply did not work. When a young friend from a neighboring town was going off to seminary with his wife, he needed a luggage rack. I told him he could have mine. He came over, fitted the thing on his car, and offered to pay me. I said, "No. Gene, let it be our gift to you." Well, this man was overcome with gratitude, aware that I was a poor preacher giving him a brand new luggage rack, used only two months. He began to carry on to his wife about what friends Bruce and Hazel Larson were, and I accepted all of this in silence, enjoying my own generosity. Finally my wife spoke up and said, "For heaven's sake, honey, tell them that the luggage rack is no good and doesn't work!"

You can guess my reaction. I wanted to disappear. Deflated as I was, nevertheless, I believe that this must happen within the Christian community. People can begin to blow the whistle on the pretensions and posturings and phony silences of others so that they can be loosed from their graveclothes and allowed to walk away as real people.

I know that many people are concerned that this kind of a confessional society might overfocus on the negative. François Fénelon lived between 1651 and 1715. He faced that problem in his day and his word is a good word for us today, as an ancient Christian to contemporary Christians.

As light increases, we see ourselves to be worse than we thought. We are amazed at our former blindness as we see issuing forth from the depths of our heart a whole swarm of shameful feelings, like filthy reptiles, crawling from a hidden cave. We never could have believed that we had harbored such things, and we stand aghast as we watch them gradually appear. But we must neither be amazed nor disheartened. We are not worse than we were; on the contrary, we are better. But while our faults diminish, the light by which we see them waxes brighter and we are filled with horror. Bear in mind, for your comfort, that we only perceive our malady when the cure begins.

Recently someone sent me this greeting: "May you always be young and glad, and even if it's Sunday, may you be wrong. For when men are always right, they are no longer young." Rigidity and defensiveness are marks of old age. This greeting captures the good news about the new society of those who have come to know Jesus and who walk in the light with their brothers and who, therefore, are eternally young.

# The Jesus Style

One day a few months ago I was flying from Toronto to Vancouver. In Winnipeg a woman about my age got on and took the seat next to me. She promptly engaged me in conversation, most of which was about her daughter. The daughter, nineteen at that time, had dropped out of school, renounced all of her parents' values, put her belongings in a pack, and gone off to bum around Europe indefinitely. When the woman finished telling me this long story, she asked, "Where did we fail her?"

I am finally learning not to answer those kinds of questions, even though it is perversely satisfying to do so. Embarrassed at having talked so much, the woman then asked me what I did for a living. I told her I was a Presbyterian clergyman. This triggered the story of her own spiritual pilgrimage. She had been everything from Jewish to Roman Catholic and even more recently an agnostic. But now, she informed me she was attending a certain church regularly and with much interest. The preacher, it seems, was the only man of God she'd ever known who identified with his people. He did not talk down to them but believed that they had a capacity for responsible action and goodness. He made God very real by loving people as they were.

What a strange parable. Deeply influenced by a man of God who has been able to accept her as she is, the woman still sees no connection between that and the way she is relating to her daughter. With her daughter she is critical, fault-finding, judgmental, and preachy.

I believe that it is possible for a person to have responded in those three dimensions we've already discussed—the volitional, conceptual, and confessional—and still be making a mess of his life in the area of relationships. A committed Christian, doctrinally sound and walking in the light can go around turning off people, boring people, hurting people, or simply being unable to relate and love in a meaningful way.

The Bible says, "Let there be no imitation Christian love among you" (Rom. 12:9, Phillips). This is the very problem we're confronting today. The Bible does not suggest that we are imitation Christians, but rather that we are imitating Christian love.

More specifically, Jesus gives us the commandment to "love as I have loved you." He is talking about the area of relationships. Perhaps there is no better place to practice the cure of souls than in this area. I have two very dear friends, both committed Christians and married to each other. No one could fault their commitment to Christ, their devotion to do his will, their sincerity, their openness, or their responsible involvement with the world. But these two people were destroying each other, unable to relate lovingly.

This inability to love and relate is not just a problem for husbands and wives or for parents and children. It is a spiritual cancer at the very heart of some of the most dynamic churches and Christian organizations. It's tragic how sincerely committed and deeply spiritual Christians have failed in relationships.

Here is a portion of a letter sent by a gifted man of God to his board of directors several years ago.

For some years now I have been making noises for help to the staff, to the board, and to friends. I have been critical and sometimes resentful because it seemed no one heard my cries, or if they did, they wanted to give answers before they heard me out for my real inner concerns. I'm sorry for my attitude in this regard. More recently, I have been learning that much of the fault is within myself. I have represented myself as the strong one, the adequate one, the one with the answers. I have become God in many people's eyes and I have put myself there. All this has been a defense against my inner weakness and helplessness. I have been too proud to talk plainly, too proud to allow myself to be seen as weak. Well, of myself I am weak and helpless and I know it now.

I determined that I must break the false image. I can no longer live with being two people. The bind of what I ought to be and what I am is impossible to contain.

This letter ends with a resignation which precipitated a situation that still is not healed. But I can identify with that man who has been serving a board that could not hear or minister to his real needs. I can also identify with that board in their failure. They used this man and honored him without any kind of genuine ministry to him.

Our relatability to groups, as well as to individuals, seems to be the key to the preaching of the gospel in this or any age. Why is it that one particular person preaching the gospel turns you on, makes your pulse beat faster and your faith grow stronger, while another person preaching the gospel turns you off, makes you want to reject him and his message? Sometimes we even feel ashamed of being identified with that kind of gospel. Yet both men may be preaching the same gospel.

Recently I saw a group of Jesus freaks take over the microphone at a large gathering for Presbyterians in Cincinnati. These winsome young people, with their long straggly hair and ragged old clothes, simply witnessed to the power of Christ and talked about the need for a second birth. If some old revivalists had proclaimed this in the same crowd, the message would have seemed judgmental and pharisaical. Yet these young people preached the same gospel that you would hear over a hundred radio stations traveling in your car on a Sunday morning. Their gospel was powerful because of their own style. Truly, as Marshall McLuhan has said, the medium is the message. When we turn people off in our communications, it is usually because of our lack of relatability rather than because of the message we bring.

There are some ways that we can experience real relationship with people, singly or in groups. I'm going to mention ten of them, hoping that they may suggest to you something of what an authentic life style would look like in this area of creative relationships.

*1. Be real.* Jesus came to live in us so that by the power of his indwelling spirit we might become the unique persons he created us to be. Don't try to be like any other Christian you know or even like our Lord himself. Simply allow him to dwell in you and make you more fully you. Don't try to be spiritual. The Holy Spirit acting in and through people in the Book of Acts and the New Testament somehow does not make them look very spiritual, as we interpret that word today. When the angel of the Lord stands in prison with Peter, he says just three things after kicking Peter awake: "Get up. Put on your shoes and belt. Follow me." Then he leads Peter out of prison and disappears. This is angel talk! Men of faith ought to be just as earthly as that in their communications. The Bible record indicates they certainly were. Part of being real is to discover concrete ways of lifting burdens, even as our Lord did and commands us to do.

Gert Behanna, whose book *The Late Liz* has now been made into a movie, is one of God's most remarkable characters. This woman had run through three husbands, was an alcoholic, attempted suicide, and got converted in her fifties. She now travels around the country speaking to groups almost every day of the year. She is responsible for thousands of people coming to know the Lord who so changed her. When we met recently, I said, "What have you been doing lately?"

"Well," she said, "I travel around a lot, Bruce, as you know, and I used to get so disgusted about the dirty restrooms in gas stations. To go into most of them, you've got to wear galoshes. Each time I used one, I complained to the Lord about how this servant of his was being treated.

"Then one day Jesus seemed to be saying to me, 'Gert, inasmuch as you've done it unto the least of these my brethren, you have done it unto me.' I said, 'Lord, you mean you use these restrooms, too?' When I realized that he was the person who'd be coming into the gas station restroom after me, I knew I'd better do something about it. Now when I go into a messy restroom, I pick up all the towels and stuff them into the wastebasket. I take a towel and wipe off the mirror and the sink and the toilet seat. I leave the place looking as clean as possible and I say, 'Well Lord, there it is, I hope you enjoy it.'"

I think this is what love is all about. No trumpets, no fanfare, no publicity. Just do the thing that will make life better for those following after.

2. *Identify with people.* This is the whole mystery of the incarnation. Jesus left heaven and all the power and authority of being the Creator of heaven and earth and came down to be among us, as one of us totally. The thing he commands us to do is to go where people are and be among them. We must open our lives enough to let people know that we hurt and hope and feel and laugh and cry in the same ways that they do.

Most of us learn by watching rather than by hearing. So often as parents or teachers or husbands or wives or supervisors in an office, we think that we have only to tell people what to do. In point of fact, people are watching us all the time and doing pretty much what we're doing. They identify with us, so we need to be good models for them.

This whole idea of modeling is not foreign to the New Testament. Paul was anything but perfect, even after he was converted and called to be an apostle, but he tells Christians that they ought to be like him. He says, "If you're confused about what you ought to be, look at me and do what I'm doing."

Paul often failed, and Luke seems to enjoy writing up many of Paul's human imperfections. But Paul knew how to handle problems, how to deal with failures, and how to go through difficulties by the grace of God. He suggests that we can look at him and learn how to handle what life throws at us, including our own failures.

In New York City there is a legend about a man named Birch Foracker who had been the president of Bell Telephone Company. Friends of mine tell me that often, when going to or from the theater fully dressed in his evening clothes, he would leave his companions and step into a manhole in the middle of the street. Why? Because there were men down there working on emergency work and he wanted to encourage them and let them know he appreciated what they were doing on a blustery winter's night.

This is the incarnation principle. We are to go where people are hurting to let them know that we care. We are to identify some of our inner feelings and model a style of life they can copy.

3. *Listen to people.* A dear friend of mine, Mrs. Samuel Shoemaker, has a gifted secretary who helps her in her work with the Anglican Fellowship of Prayer. Their office is full of signs, but the one that grabbed my eye was one that her secretary had written with a big crayon and taped above her telephone at the desk. It said simply: "I love you enough to listen." The price of love is often intense and excruciating listening to try to hear what somebody is really saying. I have memorized an anonymous quote: "I know you believe you understand what you think I've said, but I'm not sure you realize that what you heard is not what I meant." Real listening is never easy.

The ministry of listening is rare. Can you remember the last time somebody took time to draw you out and ask you questions and listen intently? I have great difficulty loving Christian friends who, having spent two or three hours with me over lunch or dinner or in some other situation, leave saying, "Hey, next time we're together I want to hear all about you!" I know people who've been saying that for years, but the next time never comes. It's always the same. They are still telling me about all the things God is doing in and through them. When they leave, I'm just human enough to feel used and sometimes deeply resentful.

When someone comes along with whom there can be some conversational Ping-Pong, the exchange of ideas, feelings and hurts, I know that God has come to love me through that person. I am sensitive to the ministry of listening to other people because it means so much to me to be listened to.

I have learned a great deal about listening from a friend of mine who is the executive vice-president of a large insurance company. One day as we were having a retreat with a few other men, he shared some things he'd learned in his ministry to the executives under him. He said there are at least five levels of need that people feel at varying times in their lives. The first is survival. This is basic for the person who has been told that he has a fatal illness or that death is a possibility. Perhaps he has just been in an automobile accident and his chance of living is slim. Security is the second level. The person at this level is not sure that he can keep his job or earn enough money to provide for his family or their future. The third level is social, the need to belong to a group where you feel that you are "in" and cared for. The fourth level is the need for status—a bigger house, a bigger car, our name in the paper, or a promotion. People who have had their needs met on all four of these levels then become aware of the need for satisfaction, which is the last and ultimate need. This is the need for good clothes and gourmet foods, rare wines, foreign travel, and so on.

In trying to be a Christian employer and minister to the people under him, my friend had to be aware that a person on the survival or security level could not care less about the social, status, or satisfaction levels. Only as the lower level needs are being met does a person become aware of his appetites and ambitions on higher levels. So, while one day it may be very important for a colleague to have a larger ashtray for his office as a status symbol, a week later that same man may be existing on the survival level because of some doctor's diagnosis or prognosis. It is helpful for us to be aware that people's needs keep changing. We must listen for their level of need and try to be a friend at that level.

Further, the people we meet often react to us because of an association of which neither of us is aware. Returning from a conference recently, I shared my plane seat with a lovely woman who had also attended the conference. I began to realize how extremely hostile she was to me in all of our preliminary conversation. Too tired at this point to be a Christian gentleman, I simply said to her, "Listen, lady, I can't handle your hostility and your anger against me just now. I don't know what I've done, but if you can't tell me, let's call this relationship off for now, and I'll read my book and you read yours." That did it. Within a very few minutes we were able to discuss the fact that I represented all of the things she hated most in life. She had been divorced by a minister, so she hated men and she hated ministers. A European, she had had a bad experience in the war and she hated soldiers, which I had been, and Americans, which I was.

This is not an approach I recommend. But because I was simply too tired to play games, I got down to the business of hearing this person's needs. The art of listening with the ears of the Holy Spirit is essential to any relationship.

4. *Affirm people.* We are not called to minister like John the Baptist, to call forth doom and point out sins in people. We have had too much of that under the guise of preaching the gospel. Jesus has called us to

love as he loves us, and he was a very different man than his cousin John. Until the coming of Jesus, John among men was the greatest, but Jesus was a totally new creation and he calls us to be new creations with him. Jesus believed in people, affirmed them, called fishermen to be apostles, loved prostitutes, pharisees, and Samaritans. All kinds of people found hope because of Jesus' relationship to them. As Christians, this is to be our style.

In New York last year Bernard Baruch College presented an award to Anthony J. Ermillio, an elevator operator employed there for over twenty years. In fact, the entire college observed Tony Day. At a packed assembly the dean of students presented Tony with an honorary doctor of transportation degree. He said, "Tony stands for a number of things that we need, and he provides them in a very difficult setting. We need morale and he gives it. We need warmth and he gives it." The chairman of the student council read a citation which said, among other things, "When you get off the elevator, Tony says something that makes you want to go to class. He makes riding in his car one of the less dehumanizing experiences."

After accepting the award, Tony, close to tears, read an Irish blessing which he had written down for the occasion: "May the sun shine warm upon your face, may the wind be at your back, and may God hold you in the palm of his hand until we meet again."

In a school that is largely dehumanizing, as schools tend to be, one elevator operator has caught something of this affirming style of life and has become both a leaven and a light in a place that needs both.

I have a quotation by Victor Hugo on the wall of my office which says, "Man lives by affirmation even more than by bread." Jesus Christ is God's great affirmation of man. He loves us in our sins, he wants to change us, but he is totally on our side while we are yet sinners, and he calls us to enter into his great love and acceptance. When we have done this, then we go out and become this affirmation for others.

I've been making an experiment lately as I watch many TV preachers. The words are about the love of God and forgiveness for sinners, but if you turn off the sound and simply look at the gestures and the faces, or if you turn the sound low to listen to the tone of the voices, all you see and hear communicated is anger. Television preachers are not the only ones guilty of this. How often I relate to people in my home or office or in my circle of friends as a prophet who must straighten out, teach, correct, bring down wrath, point out faults. But people are not changed by the John the Baptist approach. Rather, as God through one of his people affirms their strengths, they find hope for their failures.

Recently, we found ourselves in constant conflict with one of our teenage children. When summer came, we talked to him about his need to get away and live for the summer in a different community. We told him that we knew he had charisma, destiny, and maybe even greatness in him, but that probably right now all he would get from his parents was criticism. If exposed to us too long, he would begin to believe all the things we said about him which were only partly true. He needed to be where other people could believe in him, draw him out, and affirm him. So he went, and God did, through strangers, give the affirmation this boy needed and which his parents at that point were unable to give. Sometimes we have to let our children go so that they can find the bread of affirmation and not starve to death in our very homes.

5. *Share decision-making.* Of all the things I could

say about this, I will emphasize just one thing. Certainly, to be in right relationship with people means that we honor them enough to let them in on all kinds of planning, whether it be family planning, vacation planning, financial planning, or plans for running the church or changing the world. We honor them, we love them as Christ loved us, when we let them in on the setting of goals and the determining of strategy at every level.

6. *Don't try to change people.* Again, we think of Jesus and John the Baptist. John was always trying to get people to change their way of life. Jesus wanted to change them even more, but he did not talk about change or press for change, and people came to repentance at his hands. Listen to the wise words of Paul Tournier.

> Answer ideas with ideas, but answer the person with the person. Often the heart's true response is silence. . . . The people who have helped me the most are not those who have answered my confessions with advice, exhortation or doctrine, but rather those who have listened to me in silence, and then told me of their own personal life, their own difficulties and experiences. It is this give and take that makes dialogue. If we answer with advice, exhortation or theories, we are putting ourselves in the position of superiority, not equality.[1]

Who are the people who have helped you the most when you have been in a crucial situation? I dare say it was not those who were advice-givers but people such as Paul Tournier describes. When we press for change, we are implying, however subtly, that people are not acceptable as they are.

7. *Love specifically.* By this I mean, love one person at a time and love that person in specific ways. So

many of our relationships bog down because we try to love everybody instead of taking on a few as our particular mission.

A man told me recently that his life was changed when his pastor asked him, "Whom do you love?" He replied, "Well, I love everybody." "No," the pastor pursued. "Whom do you really love right now?" "Well," he said, "I don't have any enemies." But his pastor persisted, "I'm not asking you that. I'm asking you to tell me one person specifically by name that you are now involved in loving in a particular way." Well, the fact that this man could think of no one led to a genuine change in his own life. He discovered that it takes a new dimension of commitment to love one person specifically rather than to love all humanity generally and to have no enemies.

Jesus primarily loved twelve people. The hundreds and thousands that he healed and taught benefited from his ministry, but the whole Kingdom of God came about through his ability to spend three years in deep relationship with twelve men. Certainly, it would be presumptuous to claim to love more than twelve people at any given time. The cure of souls is possible only as we become a person for only a few at any given point in our lives.

8. *Don't "play it safe."* Any meaningful relationship requires a high degree of vulnerability. There is risk in loving. You may be laughed at and misunderstood. You may be rejected when you say you're sorry. It's risky to be involved in the intrigue of people's lives.

There is so much theology and philosophy found in many of our comic strips today. One of my favorites is Andy Kapp. In the strip several years ago, I remember Flo, the wife of this English cockney n'er-do-well pacing the floor of the living room looking worried.

In the next picture she's standing with her arms crossed thinking. She says, "Tch! Three whole days without speaking. This is ridiculous." In the next picture she walks up to Andy with a smile and says, "I'm sorry I acted like I did . . . you were in the right. Friends?" Andy, nonplused, says, "O.K., friends," puts on his coat, and starts to walk out. In the next picture, as he walks by her, Flo puts her arms around him and plants a big wet mushy kiss on his cheek, and Andy looks surprised and says nothing. As he steps outside the house, he meets one of his cronies, who says, "I 'eard that, Andy. It takes a good woman to apologize when she's in the wrong." And as they're walking off down the street together, Andy says, "It takes a better one to apologize when she's *not*."

This is the very stuff of redemptive, creative relationships. It means, right or wrong, being willing to say, "I am sorry," and you know how costly this is, especially when it's someone about whom you care deeply.

Getting involved in any creative kind of Christian team in your church, in a small group, or in some ad hoc task force is just as costly. People who are converted and working together as Christians are just like non-Christians in terms of tensions, touchiness, and hostilities. Look at the Apostle Paul's relationships with his teammates. Anger, jealousy, bragging, and all the rest are a part of New Testament life, and they are a part of church life today.

Betty O'Connor, in her excellent book, *Eighth Day of Creation*, says that no Christian team can go very far in living out life together until it deals with the whole business of jealousy. Jealousy between mature Christian teammates? You bet! So many of us are afraid of this happening that we hold back and never enter into this kind of life. But this is only part of the price of loving. There is another kind of fear that must be faced as we risk being vulnerable, and that is the fear of being imperfect. Nothing will reveal your imperfections more than being part of a Christian team or a small group. Listen to what St. Francis de Sales said about this.

It is not possible that the Spirit of God should dwell in the mind that wishes to know too much of what is happening within itself. . . . You are afraid of being afraid. Then you are afraid of being afraid of being afraid. Some vexation vexes you, then you are vexed at being vexed by that vexation. In the same way I have often seen people who, having lost their temper, are afterwards angry at having been angry. All this is like the circles made when a stone is cast into the water . . . first a little circle forms, then that in its turn makes a bigger one, and that one makes another.

The answer is not to find some esoteric life in the Spirit that will prevent these things from happening. To love any person deeply or to enter into the life of a team at any level means that these things will happen. We must not be surprised when they do. God is with us as we go through them, and we can find his answers to them.

9. *Ask for help.* Be willing to receive from other people. Perhaps this is one of the most immediately recognizable signs of good leadership today and certainly one of the marks of Jesus' own life style among us. He was always asking people for food, for water, for help, for companionship, for all kinds of things.

I know a man in a Texas town whose life has been radically changed because he launched into an area in which he had no expertise. A Southern Baptist deacon, lay witness, converted businessman, he was asked, along with a number of other businessmen, by the president of the United States to help employ unemployables. The request came during a trip to Washington, and he prayed about it for some time. He said to himself, "I don't know any unemployables in our town. I don't know how to help them." But he began to find out who these neighbors were. He asked for help from them. Then he went to his fellow manufacturers and employers in his own town to ask for their help. The end result has been twofold. First, thousands of unemployables have been employed in that town because of the pioneer efforts of this one man. Second, he has become a new person in relationships because he dared to move into an area in which he had no expertise and could openly ask for help.

This is a new posture for a lot of us and one that can lead to maturity.

*10. Love in terms meaningful to the other.* Give what is wanted, not what you enjoy giving. Stop to ask yourself whether the person you are trying to love wants the specific kind of help or gift or ministry that you find so satisfying to give. Instead, try to ask yourself what it is that would convey to the other person in unmistakable ways that he is loved and cared for by you at that very moment.

I will never forget one spring day several years ago when I had planned to go flounder fishing in Raritan Bay off the Jersey coast with my two boys. That morning at breakfast, I discovered that the boys were involved either in Saturday jobs or other plans. When they had both left, my wife said, "Honey, I'd like to go fishing with you." Well, she sometimes likes fishing, but on a cold, windy spring day out on the bay? No way! So I protested. When she insisted, I said, "No, you don't really want to go. You're just feeling sorry for me." But she said, "No, it would be great fun." And so we went out and had one of the great days of our life. I was loved by my wife in a way that was especially meaningful to me. This is what love is all about in any situation with any person or group of people. How many Christian couples need to discover how to stop loving one another spiritually and how to become real people, lovers and friends, one to another.

I treasure a letter that a couple sent me several years ago. Here is part of it.

Dear Bruce,

Your remark to us that God is even more concerned about our sex life than about our prayer life was a completely new idea to me. I felt it was true and it has been flashing off and on for me in neon lights ever since then. If I'm out to please God, then I'd better give my best to that sex life! Well, if you should ask us again, "How is your sex life?", you wouldn't get any cool, just-fine answer. It *was* good and it *was* just fine, but now, it is great, simply great.

The letter goes on to describe some of the changes these two have found in each other with God's help.

What is the end product when we begin to live in relational wholeness? We find out what love is all about, and, in the process, we discover what it means to be real. One of the great children's books is *The Velveteen Rabbit*. Here is a wonderful bit of dialogue between a new toy rabbit in the nursery and an old skin horse.

"What is REAL?" asked the Rabbit one day, when they were lying side by side. "Does it mean having things that buzz inside you and a stick-out handle?"

"Real isn't how you're made," said the Skin Horse. "It's a thing that happens to you. When a child loves you for a long, long time, not just to play with, but REALLY loves you, then you become Real."

"Does it hurt?" asked the Rabbit.

"Sometimes," said the Skin Horse, for he was always truthful. "When you are Real you don't mind being hurt."

"Does it happen all at once, like being wound up, or bit by bit?"

"It doesn't happen all at once. You become. It takes a long time—that's why it doesn't often happen to people who break easily or have sharp edges or have to be carefully kept. Generally, by the time you are Real, most of your hair has been loved off, and your eyes drop out and you get loose in the joints and very shabby. But these things don't matter at all because once you are Real, you can't be ugly, except to people who don't understand."[2]

## 6

# It's O.K. to Be Angry

The *New Yorker* magazine printed a cartoon some years ago that I have never forgotten and over which I still chuckle. Two men are standing on a street corner across from a church. It is obviously Sunday noon and people are pouring out of the church, cheering, laughing, arms in the air, some dancing. In the middle of all this they are carrying out their be-robed preacher on their shoulders. Observing this, one man says to the other, "I wonder what he preached on?"

I suspect this cartoon stays with me because I would like to be a preacher who could turn people on like that. I would like to be one of the worshipers under a preacher like that. I would like the church itself to be a place where such genuine feelings can be released.

Feelings are powerful forces, elusive, hard to understand, and with roots so obscure that most of us are unaware of them. While the emotions are certainly involved to a greater or lesser degree in at least three of the other areas we have discussed—the volitional, the confessional, and the relational—they are also a separate dimension of our pie of wholeness which must be understood and dealt with as we practice the cure of souls. We need to understand something of the

85

subterranean forces that occupy all of our personal basements and which sometimes flood up into the attic and out the windows of our lives to touch and ignite others, both positively and negatively.

In 1966 the Southern Presbyterian Church in the United States, aware of this growing need for understanding the emotional needs of men, published a study made by a number of psychologists, psychiatrists, doctors, and clergymen. Listen to their definition of emotional illness:

> Emotional illness may be defined as that state characterized (singly or in combination) by diminished confidence or pleasure in one's physical self, by a diminished or absent sense of meaning or purpose, by rigidity and stereotyped response to all of life's contingenices, or by a relatively hopeless attitude toward life and other people. These factors, alone or in combination, effectively impede or prevent abundant living in the three critical areas of love, work and play.[1]

If this is an accurate definition, there are many people in our churches, converted and doctrinally sound, who are suffering from emotional illness.

Perhaps the church has a special need to study the area of emotions in light of certain pioneer discoveries now being made by psychologists. Men, like the controversial R. D. Laing in England, are suggesting on the basis of much clinical evidence that the good people tend to break down emotionally and wind up with schizophrenia. People who can let their feelings out, who can risk making enemies or who can bluster around looking stupid and foolish, are less prone to emotional illness and schizophrenia than people who are even dispositioned and exemplary in their behavior.

If this thesis interests you, I would suggest that you read Laing's book *The Divided Self*. It's not a proven theory but it does tend to explain why the church needs to explore the area of the emotions. We need to be reminded that the church is not for good people but for sick people who can acknowledge their illness and in fellowship become priests one of another. Until this takes place, we are still going to attract nice people or the emotionally rigid to our churches, and they are going to have tremendous needs in the area of emotions.

Comedy writers have an especially strong understanding of emotions. They can put their finger on those traits which are universal, and we identify with their characters and laugh. One of my favorite writers of humor is Peter DeVries. His newest book *Into Your Tent I'll Creep* has just been released, and one of my children hurried down to the bookstore to buy it for me for Christmas. The hero describes his wife during one of their disagreements in this way:

> The off and on switches in her mood, the short term swings at unpredictable reactions, had nothing to do with response or lack of it to what you were saying, or even to what she was saying, but were apparently emotional cycles going on inside her, independent of the conversation. These seemed to have their own rotation times, determined by a sort of internal chemical clock. Either that or dictated by what she was privately thinking. We all have this scenario going on inside us, more or less tied to the one going on outside—more with some people, less with others, like Miss Piano (his wife) at least a good part of the time.²

Many of us are just like Miss Piano. So much of the friction at official board meetings can be traced to this particular syndrome in all of us rather than to differences in ethics, theology, or methods of handling financial problems. A comment from somebody starts up a tape of some previous emotion, positive or negative, in someone else, and this begins to affect the entire group and the discussion. The emotion evoked may have nothing to do, actually, with what's being said or being decided. It is helpful to be aware of this dynamic in any group or meeting.

I identify with Peter DeVries's hero and his wife in his description of reactions that seem to have nothing to do with the scene being played. Recently, my wife and I were at a conference. We were getting dressed for the morning meeting. She was in the bathroom fixing her hair and I was in the bedroom. I switched on the television and all I could find were some early morning cartoons. I am inordinately fond of cartoons and so I began to watch them while I was dressing. After a few minutes, Hazel said, "Do you have to watch cartoons?" "Well, there's nothing else on," I replied. "Besides, what's wrong with cartoons?" Then she began to tell me what's wrong with cartoons, and I began to defend cartoons and so went our creative morning until we realized that what was going on had nothing to do with cartoons at all. The emotional relationship at that point was a carry-over from something that had happened the night before, too painful to talk about. It all came out over cartoons.

Unless we understand something of what is going on in our emotions, it is hard to find healing. We pray about symptoms rather than causes. I end up complaining to God about my wife, "Why is she so critical about cartoons? Help her to see that they are harmless." Or else, "Help me to overcome my childish love of cartoons." Seemingly simple disagreements can produce an awful lot of emotional baggage because we have been avoiding some of the deeper issues.

We have so many uncreative ways of handling our feelings. There is, first of all, the neurotic way. I am speaking here of the classic neurotic who is all feelings. This person does only what he feels like doing, no more, no less. He swings from mood to mood, is usually uncreative, sometimes alcoholic and given to excesses. Feelings dominate. This person expects conversion to be a new level of feeling that will make having faith and living a life of love and service a tremendous feeling trip. Of course, this is why the neurotic often falls away shortly after his conversion. His feelings don't affirm the fact that he is converted and living a life of discipleship.

In the past the church took seriously man's need for an emotional shot-in-the-arm. Think of all the twice-a-year revival services that used to be held, the successor of the annual camp meeting in our country's frontier days. Twice a year a person could have an emotional orgy, confessing guilt, making a new commitment, and being saved. This is not necessarily a bad thing and perhaps may be healthier than much of our emotionally sterile religion today. But in practicing the cure of souls as we do the cure for bodies, we try to measure the medicine needed for each person. There are some people who already emphasize their feelings too much. There are others who are so constipated in the area of feelings that they need a deep emotional release, such as the old-time revivals used to offer and in some places still do.

In the first category, the neurotic, let me put people like myself who are members of "emotions anonymous." We are people who love to wallow in feelings, who feel depressed or elated with no in-between.

When we become Christians, we emphasize strongly our belief that faith has to do with facts and acts not with squishy emotions or gooey feelings. We are very much like ex-alcoholics who now preach temperance sermons and fight John Barleycorn because, by doing so, we are saving our own sobriety. For years I have been an antifeeling person and preached it to others because I knew what the excesses led to in my own life.

Over against the neurotic who is all feelings, we find a much larger group of people who have, for a number of reasons, a negative reaction to feelings or an inability to feel. This is often the unblessed, elder-brother type who is so duty oriented and who has so little sense of self-esteem that any kind of emotion, positive or negative, is unconsciously abhorrent and repressed.

A friend of mine who comes from a large family is one of these stable, unemotional, steady, reliable types. I cannot imagine this person expressing great anger or great passion. In his family he was the fourth of eight children, and he still recalls poignantly his surprise and pleasure when one day, while he was hoeing the garden, his dad called him by his first name. In his memory that had not happened before. People like this have been so conditioned by their parents that any kind of deep feeling becomes difficult. They tend to deny their cellar impulses.

There is a third kind of person who tends to avoid any negative feelings. He has been told by parents, teachers, preachers, or someone else along the way that "good boys and girls never get angry" or that "Christians never lose their temper" or that "people won't like you if you are not good-natured." At some point in life, when he was eight or twelve or fourteen, he was suddenly overwhelmed by legitimate feelings of anger, perhaps against his mother or his father. Since he had been taught to believe that negative feelings are bad, he has to hide these feelings immediately. He tells himself that he doesn't hate, that he feels only love. Now, everyone experiences ambivalent feelings. You cannot love someone without at times hating him too. This is part of the human situation. But, never having learned this, some people feel that any acknowledgment of hate indicates an eradication of love and so they stifle their hate. They are tragically unaware that their positive feelings are also being stifled.

The feeling box down in our emotional cellar is such that when you put a great heavy concrete lid over the opening to keep out the negative feelings you are also keeping out all of your positive feelings. This results in an inability to express any passion or to initiate love. It almost seems that we are able to love and care in proportion to our ability to express anger. We must be free to hate in order to be free to love.

I know a couple who recently came to an experience of healing in this area. They both became Christians in a small group a few years ago and were living out lives of commitment, study, involvement. However, the man, a very rugged outdoor type, was still unable ever to initiate any kind of affection toward his wife and their many children. When I asked him about this in front of his wife, he said with tears in his eyes, "My wife and children are everything in the world to me. Beyond that I have nothing other than God. But I cannot say or even show how I feel."

Later in our conversation, he shared two incidents from his youth. When he was twelve years old, his father had done some outrageously unfair things. First of all, his father had forced him to kill a pet he loved because the father considered the animal a nuisance. On another occasion he was punished with extreme severity for something of which he was innocent. At that point he remembers vowing in the midst of the beating, "He'll never get to me." Well, his father never did get to him. Never again did his father have the power to make this man angry. That little boy grew up, married a woman he loved, and had children he loved. But he was unable to express his love for them because he was also unable to be angry with them. Later, in the warmth and fellowship of a group of Christians, he was able to face some of this and begin to be a person who could feel again and express the positive as well as the negative.

I am convinced this is not an unusual case. How many committed people sitting in our churches are unable to love those closest to them? We have the keys in our hands to unlock each other.

A dear friend in New England lives with her husband and her aged mother. One day this woman confided to her small group that she was angry with her mother for something that had occurred the week before. Then she quickly added, "But mother is so dear, one of the greatest people in the world. It was wrong of me to be angry and I love her deeply." At this point someone in the group said, "You mean you've never been angry with your mother before?" "Oh, no," replied Alice. The group then began to explore this with Alice, saying things like "This is not natural. If you love someone deeply as you do a husband or a child or a parent, there must be times when you are angry." "It sounds to me," one man said, "as though your mother did something when you were a girl that produced so much anger that you stifled it and have never dared to be angry with her again." When the group persisted, Alice remembered a time when her mother had humiliated her in front of a boyfriend and shortly after forced her to break her engagement. Her anger had never been expressed until that group meeting.

I had a letter from Alice recently telling of her new freedom to feel anger and resentment. She still lives with her husband and her mother and has found a new kind of love for her mother.

So often the church deals with people like Alice in just the opposite way. We look at people who are never angry and we say, "Wonderful. You are like Jesus. Jesus was never angry." And we confirm somebody in their emotional illness by our praise and admiration. Beyond praising the illness, we often ordain it and make people like this deacons, elders, trustees, and preachers. By the power of the Holy Spirit within our Christian fellowship, we need to allow people who have never been angry before to discover that it's O.K. to be angry, it's O.K. to have negative feelings.

Just before the writing of this chapter, my wife and I had one of our occasional disagreements. It was a bit more violent than usual and ended with a great unresolved issue. After a bit, we began to make up and talk. I asked Hazel to forgive me because of the strong emotions I had expressed on this issue. Then she said a liberating thing to me, "Whenever we have a disagreement, you always vent your feelings, but as soon as I begin to tell you how angry you make me, you cut me off. Don't I have the right to express how angry I feel about you without being stopped?" I suddenly realized that I had done this for years and I apologized. Then I said, "O.K., tell me how you feel about me on this issue and I promise I'll keep still and try to understand." There were several minutes of very heated language, but by the time she ran down and got her feelings out, we could both laugh. And beyond that, the issue that had caused the quarrel was no longer a problem, I've even forgotten what it was.

For too long in our married life I insisted that my wife stifle her hostile feelings because in my insecurity I couldn't handle them. Within the church, in small groups, committees, and board meetings we do the same thing. When somebody really becomes angry, we are so threatened by it that we close them off or humiliate them. Sometimes we even suggest prayer as a way of cutting them off. We find ourselves praising those people who never get angry because these people don't threaten us.

The Bible takes the whole area of emotions and feelings very seriously. Jesus did have legitimate anger from time to time, and it's recorded in the Gospels. In the Epistles we find this verse: "Don't let the sun go down on your anger." The fact that we feel anger is taken for granted, but we are to let it come out where it can be dealt with before the day ends. This is really sound psychology, and why not? It comes from the Creator of all life and of all feelings.

The Old Testament speaks of King David, of all people, as a "man after God's own heart." Why? Because although he is a constant sinner, he is free, like the old revivalists at those camp meetings, to find forgiveness and salvation all over again. He is free to confess his sins before God *and* man, and he is also free to let his feelings out and dance for joy before the ark and before his people, celebrating God's grace.

He acted much as the prodigal son must have when he came home and found his father loving and forgiving. He ate with his friends off the fatted calf, and dancing was in order. How much we need this emotional release in the church. I think God is saying, "Come dance with me. If you really hear the good news that I am offering you in Jesus Christ, come and dance with me the dance of life, with all of those who are redeemed, blessed, healed."

What, then, should we do with our feelings, as Christians and as people?

*1. Don't deny that you have either negative or positive feelings.* Remember that there are no good or bad feelings, just good or bad acts. One doesn't have to do everything his feelings prompt, but one should never deny the presence of those feelings. All true feelings need some kind of expression. If we seal our feelings too tightly, or deny them, our emotional energy will emerge sideways and obliquely. This is dishonest. This means that a wife may get the anger that her husband does not dare to vent to his boss at work.

Pent-up feelings get turned inward and begin to work against a person's well-being. Repressed feelings can lead to all kinds of mental and physical disorders.

In our relationships the expression of negative feelings can often lead to a whole new start. One of our children had never been able to say anything negative, but he seemed also to be a withholder of love. One day when he was pushed to the limit, he was able to say that he hated his mother and me. By God's grace, we could handle that. Within twelve hours, because of his expression of hatred and our acceptance of his expression of hatred, he was able to say for the first time some positive things. Since that expression of the negative, he has shown a new ability to be extravagant emotionally and to express love.

2. *Don't depend on your feelings.* This is neurotic and unhealthy and will cut the nerve of real Christian action. If we are to love people as Jesus loved them and begin to change the world, we must not depend on our feelings. We follow God's commands and love in costly ways that often don't feel good.

I mentioned earlier that I am a feeling-aholic. This means that I used to depend on my feelings. Now I am learning to evaluate my emotions a little better. In talking to a woman recently, I began to feel a sense of resentment and animosity toward her. If I had depended on my feelings, I would have terminated that relationship quickly because I couldn't handle my negative emotions. But since I am now trying not to let my feelings dictate my actions, I could continue the conversation. Before the day was over, I realized that this woman reminded me of somebody for whom I had deep hostility which I had never before expressed. As we conversed, this woman was getting emotional mail that was not addressed to her, a whole body of content and feeling that should have gone to another years ago. In talking to her, I was able to let God deal with this old resentment in me. She and I were able to move on to a creative relationship. When we don't depend on our feelings, we can stay in a relationship even when negative emotions are aroused. To hang in there is to go on faith.

3. *Don't just verbalize your feelings; actually feel your feelings.* One of my dear friends and colleagues has had a great release. She is one of those good people who was always trying to please. Some years ago,

after her rather dramatic conversion, she became aware of a great deal of unexpressed anger. She talked about this anger, particularly against her parents, and more recently, a group of caring Christians has helped her physically and verbally act out those negative emotions in a role-playing situation. She has come through this with a new ability to love and appreciate her parents.

*4. Remember that it's O.K. to feel.* Remember that there are no good feelings or bad feelings, just feelings. Loving, which is the command Christ gives us, is easier when our feelings, be they negative or positive, are not hidden.

# Listen to Your Body

Not long ago I attended a luncheon meeting at a large state hospital. The doctors and medical students present were mostly church members. We had come together to talk about healing. The question of spiritual healing came up, and someone asked if I believed in it. I said I did because God had caught my attention in this area many years ago. It happened during my days as a seminary student when I was serving a small parish on the Hudson River.

One of the parishioners, a woman named Elsie, had a tremendous faith in Christ and a firsthand experience of his power to heal. Elsie had been hospitalized following an injury and one Saturday night as I made my usual weekend rounds, she greeted me by climbing out of bed and getting onto her crutches.

"Follow me," she said, and as we walked down the hospital corridor together, she told me about a young man who had been in a coma for six days. He'd been racing his car down a local road at more than one hundred miles per hour when the car hit some obstacle and crashed. He had not recovered consciousness.

Elsie had been visiting with the young man's mother. She was from another city and the family priest had not been able to visit the hospital. Elsie assured the mother that when I came I would see her son and pray for his healing.

This terrified me. Up to that point I had not believed that the Lord who healed in the New Testament days was available for healing today. But what could I do? Elsie introduced me to the mother—who, by the way, spoke almost no English—and said cheerily, "Here is my preacher; he will pray for your son."

A nurse was on duty beside the young man's bed, an excellent nurse but one who had previously exhibited a great mistrust and dislike for Christians in general and for clergymen in particular!

There we were, a hostile nurse, a mother who could not communicate, a boy in a coma who could not hear and a scared young seminary student. The conditions for healing seemed all wrong. The only thing God had going for him was one woman who believed. As we approached the bed, Elsie said, "Here he is, pray for him."

I remember that I first prayed silently, asking God to help me know what to do. Next, I laid my hands on the boy's foot and said something like, "Lord Jesus, we know that you are here and we ask you to heal this young man."

Before the prayer was over, the boy opened his eyes and said to me, "Hi, Charlie." I mumbled that I wasn't Charlie, but that I was a friend and glad to see him.

Of the people in that room only Elsie was not surprised. She said, "Well, that's over. Let's go now." I followed her out the door, almost unable to walk.

Chuckling over this story, several of the doctors began to recount similar stories of how God got their attention in the area of spiritual healing while they were still unbelievers.

Then one doctor said, "I believe in spiritual healing, but what irks me is people who go around wanting to pray for everyone to get well." He went on to explain, "I am thinking of a woman who came back from a Christian conference some months ago where she had been healed of arthritis through prayer. Now she wants to run all over the church and my hospital praying for people to get well, and I resent it."

In the lively discussion that followed, the question was raised, "Why do we resent this kind of person who tries to force spiritual healing on everyone?" We finally concluded that this approach violates personhood. Jesus did not seek out people to heal. They came to him and asked for healing for themselves, for a friend, or for a member of the family. None were refused. The only time Jesus initiated healing was at the pool of Bethesda. Even then he asked, "Do you want to be healed?"

Our conversation about spiritual healing and the medicine of the whole person ended with this self-appraising question: "What is distinctive about a Christian doctor, as contrasted to a good doctor who is not a Christian?" Our humble consensus was that a Christian has no special medical skills that are unavailable to other colleagues, except for prayer.

But beyond that, we began to see that in many situations we clergymen and physicians are like the woman who went about determined to heal people by her prayers, violating the personhood of many, though used of God to bring healing to some. We can do the same kind of harm. By using medical skills doctors can impose healing on people who do not want to be well. For some people sickness can be an escape from life or a way to handle life, a way to justify themselves or to manipulate others.

Even Jesus did not force people to become well, and this should not be the role of the doctor or the spiritual healer. Rather, the role of the Christian is to build a relationship with sick people, whether they come willingly or reluctantly for treatment. The Christian doctor ought to be uniquely aware of the inviolate right of the human soul and will for self-determination. He ought to be able to love in such a way that patients can respond to him and to God by saying, "Yes, I do want to be well." Then the doctor is free to use all the skills at his disposal to bring healing.

To me, our discussion at that luncheon meeting embodies some of the exciting new aspects of the physical dimension of life. Even doctors are discovering that there is something more important than health.

Medical men today are pretty much agreed that man is made up of three parts—physical, mental, and spiritual. He is three in one and one in three and any other approach than this will be inadequate and incomplete. In other words, the doctor is not dealing with a body but with a person. The psychiatrist is not dealing with a mind and emotions but with a person. The clergyman is not ministering to a soul but to a person. When a person gets sick, more than his physical being has broken down, and a wise doctor has to treat more than physical symptoms and organs if he is to be adequate in the field of healing.

For a long time doctors who specialized in psychosomatic medicine, pioneers like Dr. Franz Alexander and Flanders Dunbar, advanced the theory that there are classic personality types associated with some major illnesses. Most clearly defined are the asthma type, the ulcer type, the migraine type, the rheumatoid arthritis type, and the cancer type. These pioneers insisted that emotional factors precipitated, or at least were associated with, many diseases. Later, other doctors turned this theory around and claimed that physical ailments were the cause of emotional disturbances or produced personality types.

Today both of these theories are up for grabs, and doctors speak with much less certainty. They are all agreed, however, that ample research has shown a definite relationship of mind, body, and spirit. Doctors know that they have only uncovered the tip of an iceberg.

In researching for an article on this subject, *New York Times* science writer Jane E. Brody found widespread agreement in the medical profession that emotional changes in a person's life can precipitate physical changes. To put it in simple terms, your mind or your emotions can make your body sick and in a tremendous variety of ways. The centuries-old belief that one can die of a broken heart or a crushed spirit has been borne out in many careful scientific studies.

All of this introduces us to the sixth and last piece of the pie of wholeness. An understanding of the physical dimension leads to a more comprehensive understanding of man and the ministry of the cure of souls. Christian people and the church at large need to deal with the body as much as with the mind and soul. We can no longer relegate the physical needs of people to doctors only. We all know that some of our physical illnesses, pains, and problems come from deeply spiritual causes.

In the revolution taking place today in the church, I am encouraged by this emphasis on the importance of the body and its relationship to spiritual things. Jesus did not seem to make a separation between the physical and the spiritual. When John the Baptist was languishing in prison and sent his disciples to his cousin Jesus to find out whether or not he really was the Messiah, the answer was very surprising. Jesus asked John's disciples to observe what they saw happening there as he interacted with people. He told them to report to John that "the lame walk, the blind see, the deaf hear, lepers are cleansed, and the poor have good news preached to them." Jesus' credentials were all based on his physical and social ministry. It is still true today that when the Holy Spirit does an authentic work through his followers, we will see physical and social changes as the proof.

The world has come to take seriously the relationship of the body to a person's thoughts and feelings. Much of the practice of the cure of souls is being done today by secular doctors rather than by Christians. At the University of Maryland Medical School, they are trying some new things in treating people with chronic skin problems. They have examined and treated two hundred eighty patients so far in this study, and 43 percent, or one hundred twenty, were so seriously ill that they had to leave their jobs. These patients are treated by a medical person, a social worker, and a vocational rehabilitation counselor. These specialists work with each patient to improve his self-image as well as to give him new work skills. Doctor Henry Robinson, who is in charge of the Division of Dermatology at the Medical School, says this: "The astounding success enjoyed by these two centers has demonstrated beyond a shadow of a doubt that rehabilitation is an essential part of dermatological therapy."[1]

One of the case studies involves a nineteen-year-old girl suffering from dermatitis to a very serious degree. When the girl's mother finally admitted that she herself had an alcoholism problem and sought medical help, her daughter's skin condition began to respond.

Our bodies are accurate spiritual barometers of what is happening to us inside in our thoughts and feelings. I used to suffer chronic colds, and through the first twenty years of my life, I could look forward to about a dozen of these a year. Since I've been a Christian, the number of colds has considerably reduced. The thing I have observed is that almost without exception, a cold follows a time of overwork and self-pity. It seems as though my body is saying, "Hear my needs. Care for me. Help me." Now I am sure that cold germs are always about in our society, and I am convinced that changes in temperature, getting chilled or overheated, are not the real causes of a cold. When I begin to need rest or just a little T.L.C., the germs are able to come in and do their work.

If this is true, then when my Christian friends see cold signs, they ought to be able to ask, "What is your body trying to say? What's your real problem?"

Studies tell us that chronic tiredness is in the same category. Exhaustion almost never comes from overwork. It comes, rather, from boredom or from the strain of trying to play a role. So, when people have some kind of physical collapse, the beloved community needs to ask what the real causes are and how they can be of help.

If we are going to minster to the whole person and practice the cure of souls, we need to hear the language of the body. The body does not lie; it is the truest barometer of what is going on inside us. Jesus certainly had the ability to read people. Seeing Nathaniel coming toward him, he can describe him perfectly though they have never met. Nathaniel was dumfounded by this and thought he was in the presence of a prophet. It is entirely possible that Jesus knew nothing more about Nathaniel than any of us could have known if we could perfect our reading of this language of the body.

A personnel director for a large firm in New York City told me about his method of hiring people. He evaluates them not by their verbal answers to questions in interviews but by observing what their bodies say about them as they sit in the chair. The battery of questions he runs through is simply a smokescreen. This friend says that he gets much better results from simply reading the applicant's unconscious body reactions during the interview.

Of course, we are all beginning to read the body in some of the more obvious ways. If you meet a man whose shoulders are drawn backward, you immediately sense a person in whom there is resistance. If you meet a person whose shoulders droop forward, he is probably under some kind of pressure or some heavy burden. If his shoulders are perfectly stiff, in a soldier-like stance, he communicates rigidity and an effort to be disciplined. On the other hand, with a person whose characteristic gesture is a shrugging of the shoulders, we can guess that he is a defeated person waiting for the next blow to fall.

Other characteristics of the body are just as revealing. The slope of our abdomens, the steadiness of our eye contact, the tightness of our mouths are all clues. And beyond the obvious are the more subtle things such as energy level, elimination, digestion, and sexual performance, all of which reveal inner attitudes and tensions.

The behavioral sciences today are studying body language and have produced a number of intriguing books. One written by William Schutz entitled *Here*

*Comes Everybody* examines body language at great length. The author, for example, has personally suffered from a sore left hip most of his life. He has finally associated this hip trouble with his inability to initiate things in life. His theory is that the left side of the body is the initiator. In marching we step out with the left foot. Boxers lead with their left hand. So Mr. Shutz sees the soreness of his left side as an unconscious unwillingness to take the initiative in social or interpersonal situations. As he has faced this and dealt with it, his sore left hip is becoming strong and healthy.

Some of our favorite expressions are also telltale signs of our inner feelings and thoughts. The words we use to show our frustration are revealing. A friend who used to work with me had suffered chronic migraines for years. When she was angry, her most frequent expression was "I wanted to blow my top." Well, migraines are literally blowing one's top! We hear other people say, "What a pain in the neck!" or "Oh, my aching back!" Chance phrases like these are often related to actual trouble spots in the body.

Jesus Christ came to reconcile each of us to God, to one another, to the world and to ourselves. Part of being reconciled to ourselves is to be reconciled to our bodies. Your body is your friend, not your enemy. When your body breaks down, it is not failing you. On the contrary, it is struggling with conflicts and decisions and carrying burdens that you have not yet been able to handle. And this is why an understanding of body language is so important.

In business, for example, when management avoids dealing with particular problems, they are pushed down to a level where the staff is forced to deal with them. When the administration and faculty of a school won't deal with controversial issues, the student body begins to deal with them, and we have all lived with the repercussions from this in recent years. In a church where the pastor and the official board do not deal with problems, the congregation has to live with them. In a society, when responsible government does not deal with problems, they move down to the grassroots and are the cause of riots and unrest. In our families, when a husband and wife cannot deal with problems adequately, the children in the family have to live with and handle these unresolved tensions.

This is also true in the physical dimension. If you cannot deal with resentments, unhealed relationships, hidden sins, these are repressed until your body becomes the one who must deal with them. This is the whole premise of psychosomatic medicine. Your body becomes one who suffers for you so that you can continue to exist in spite of tremendous unresolved problems.

I spoke about this on the West Coast recently, and at the close of the lecture someone came up with this response, "I suddenly realize that my body is a Christ-type. It is literally suffering and dying to give me more time to respond maturely to certain life situations. I am beginning to genuinely love my body and to be grateful for all it is bearing that my mind and spirit cannot face."

If your body is your best friend and suffering for you, we in the church need to take each other's physical problems seriously. It seems unfortunate that people with alcohol problems have had to go outside their own church to Alcoholics Anonymous. Overweight people have to find help from Weight Watchers. I thank God for these groups that are helping people to deal with their physical problems. But if the body is our friend, a part of our spirit and mind, then the church must have a ministry to the body, too. We need to say to one another, "Why do you have that cold?" or "Why are you tired all the time?" or "Why are you overweight?" "Can we help?" And we can begin a ministry to the body as part of our total ministry.

We need to understand that not only can the spirit make the body sick, but the body can affect the spirit was well. Psychosomatic medicine is based upon a profound truth—the body and the spirit are a unity. As we begin to work with the body, make it a friend, listen to it, make it stronger and healthier, we will have a new doorway to the soul.

We're talking about something more important than physical health. We are talking about health for the whole person. The psychologist Rollo May has said, "It's very unhealthy to worship mere health. We mustn't produce adjustment at the expense of sensitivity and other things we ought to value more."[2] So this sixth piece of the pie, the physical, is a part of God's total plan. In an attempt to use God to restore health, we can miss what our body is saying to us about the whole person.

I feel certain that the lay apostolate emerging now in the church is going to become part of a whole new healing force. The healing team will be made up of doctors, psychiatrists, clergymen, and lay counselors. Abraham Maslow says, "Face to face therapy is a luxury. It's too slow and too expensive. It's not the right answer if you think, as I shamelessly do, in terms of changing the whole world. We need more shortcuts. We have to teach everyone to be a therapist. A lot more people might be therapeutic than you might think they have it in them to be."[3]

On the secular scene, then, this great leader in the

medicine of the whole person is giving a mandate to everyone, and especially to us in the church, to move boldly into the area of understanding the body, befriending it and making it part of our love and concern.

## 8

# Sexy Christians

I've encountered many mature, responsible Christians these days who are reading books about sex. One couple, following directions in one of the latest volumes, was trying to discover new erogenous zones. "Kissing my wife's big toe probably would have worked," the husband reported, "if we both hadn't started laughing!"

I think this new and acceptable kind of interest in sex is a healthy change for most of us Christians. There is no one who needs to be more enlightened about sex than those of us who have had a Christian upbringing. We have all been victims of a lot of wrong thinking. I think this accounts for the tremendous interest in a variety of new books on the subject. The little volume *Everything You Always Wanted to Know About Sex . . . But Were Afraid to Ask* has literally flooded the country, and for a good reason. That book and a number of companion volumes about "him," "her," and "them" has found a wide audience among all kinds of people—young, middle-aged, and older—including the most serious Christians. Beyond that, the simple issue of sex education in the public schools has caused a furor everywhere, even in the most enlightened communities. If you have attended any of these local school board meetings, then you

111

know that our feelings about sex are strong, our ignorance on the subject is vast and often hidden under the guise of faith and morality.

The purpose of this chapter is to explore the sexual dimension of life from a Christian perspective. If you are concerned about practicing the cure of souls, then you must be able to relate to another person as he or she struggles with his or her sexuality. I have not made the sexual dimension a separate piece of our pie of wholeness because this dimension of life spills over and touches our entire personality. As a matter of fact, it involves every one of the sections of the pie that we have looked at so far.

It seems to me that currently there are three basic views of sex, two of them widespread and basically unhealthy. First, sex is a necessary evil. In the church we have seen this as a glorification of celibacy as over against the married state. The implication is that if one were really "Christian," he could live with a minimum of sex in his life or none at all. It's surprising to find this ancient philosophy popping up today on the secular scene. Ratings for movies are determined by the degree of nudity portrayed. A movie showing a bare breast or bottom becomes an R movie even though there may be no overt sex or violence in it. But a movie full of violence and implicit sex may get a PG rating, providing there is no nudity.

A second point of view maintains that sex is a simple biological function and meant to be enjoyed. In classic literature (books like *The Decameron* and *Canterbury Tales*) we find much in the medieval and eighteenth-century traditions that would indicate great numbers of people practicing uninhibited, bawdy sex. In more recent times the Playboy philosophy is a very sophisticated presentation of irresponsible sex. Intercourse is to be enjoyed just as one enjoys a meal, a bath, or a good night's sleep.

The seeds of this kind of sexual liberation were sown by Freud who reacted, and rightly, against the Victorian view that sex was a necessary evil and therefore to be repressed. Freuds theory that man suffered neuroses because he could not give free rein to his sexual drives has done irreparable harm, especially to Christians who have sought new attitudes through psychoanalysis.

There is a third view of sex especially applicable for Christians which is that sex is good and to be enjoyed but always in the context of responsibility. Christians ought to be sexy. Sex is not a necessary evil but a gift given by God to enjoy. God has also given certain rules that make us responsible for others and for ourselves. Within these confines, sex is a powerful and wonderful gift to be celebrated.

In helping someone else find all that he is meant to be by God in the area of sexuality, it helps to understand which of these three basic attitudes is his. To help a person change his basic attitude about sex is more important than to help him solve a particular problem in this area.

There is another dimension of sex which is undergoing drastic change in our time. This is the distinction between sex and personhood. In our society our sex determines our culturally assigned role. There are male and female virtues, male and female talents, male and female reactions, all predetermined. In point of fact, we have assumed there is a basic male personality and a basic female personality.

What is the biblical view of the male/female role? Certainly God created two sexes, male and female, and called them good and meant them for one another. In the Old Testament and even in the New, the woman's role is clearly defined as inferior to that of the man. But I think we need to understand that the revelation came at a time when slavery was acceptable, Samaritans were judged inferior, and live animals were killed to placate God. All of this occurred simply because man did not know any better.

How amazing that Paul, at the same time he speaks of women being silent in church and submissive to men, also says, by the inspiration of the Holy Spirit, that in Christ there is neither male nor female, only a new creation. I'm not sure Paul even knew what he was saying, but I believe with all my heart that he was prophetic in speaking of the time to come when we stop assigning certain personality roles to sexes. We are finally beyond trying to make a left-handed child right-handed, so we ought to stop assuming that a boy who is basically aesthetic or artistic or gentle is not a man. In the same way women who are basically aggressive, competent managers, and organizers should not be made to feel that they are less than feminine.

This strict assignment of roles to the sexes may account for the great number of people who become homosexuals or lesbians. A man feels so ashamed of being effeminate that he stops competing with men and enters into a female world. The same can be true for a woman. It would be far healthier, it seems to me, were we to suggest that there might be a creative union between a female with male tendencies and a male with female tendencies. In point of fact I know a number of couples like this who seem to have mature and healthy marriages.

In our own marriage my wife is more capable of handling certain matters which are traditionally considered the male prerogative (checkbook and income taxes). At first it was difficult to accept this and not feel threatened. But liberation is coming and it feels good for me not to have to maintain my maleness but to be a person married to a person and to enjoy both our personhood and our sexuality and our different gifts.

Let's look now at some of the questions that come up in the area of sex. In thinking about the cure of souls, let's explore some of the most common areas of concern and see how we can view ourselves and others in the light of God's potential for each one of us.

*1. What about premarital sex?* This is the question I am asked most commonly today in meetings with young people. In our age of so-called sexual liberation this question is bound to come up. In the past the church's main arguments against premarital sex were the risk of pregnancy and venereal disease. Since science has removed these two threats, we are now obliged to find a genuinely biblical reason for chastity.

When I grew up, it was assumed that premarital sex was as wrong as adultery and that the Bible explicitly said so. The Bible is clear about adultery, but it does not seem to be as explicit about premarital sex. It does say, however, that any time two people have intercourse, these two people become one in body, mind, and spirit. Far from being dirty or evil, sex at the point of intercourse is so powerful that you become one with another person. The obvious implication is that one cannot have this experience with many people, or even with several people, without violating himself as well as the other. This seems to me an implicit case for premarital chastity.

Many people have been sold on the idea of premarital sex in order to avoid coming to the honeymoon as an amateur. If the purpose of a honeymoon is for two experts to come and demonstrate their techniques on the other, then I suppose this would make sense. But I think the most exciting thing about a honeymoon is that two people come together as amateurs and learn together what it means to become one body, one mind and one spirit. If this is true, then experience works against the whole wonder of what God has planned for a marriage.

Interestingly, I have never talked to a single married couple who said they were grateful for their premarital experience. Marriage is a time for learning together how to please one another and how to fulfill one another. No amount of experience can prepare you for this.

2. *What about sex in marriage?* Marriage is more than sex but any marriage that does not include an active and healthy sex life is in trouble. Sex is more than a physical experience although it is certainly totally physical. Even a book like Masters and Johnson's that explores so much about sex and orgasm and fulfillment seems to put sex in a very spiritual category. For example, every time they report a couple having a breakthrough in the sexual area of their marriage, you find that it involves some kind of vulnerability on the part of one or both. In other words, the book seems to affirm what every Christian ought to know—that sex is not the key to union but an expression of union. God intended for a man and a woman to live together in union; in the Christian culture this means marriage. The sex act is not the means to union but rather an expression of the psychic, spiritual, emotional, and mental unity in which people hold no more secrets from each other. I can think of a number of couples who have had breakthroughs in their marriage and subsequently in their sex lives when they

could experience confession and openness with each other. When psychic walls come down, sex becomes a sacramental expression of union.

3. *What positions are permissible for intercourse in marriage?* I personally believe that there is no position that two people can use in making love that is off limits except where one of the persons feels violated or imposed upon or embarrassed. In other words, there is no accepted position. We do the thing that will bring fulfillment to the other.

I'm always suspicious when someone asks about positions in a marriage counseling situation. It seems to me that if one party can find an off-limit position, then he or she can nail the other for being "perverted." Once we begin to be legalistic in any area, the marriage becomes a very shaky affair.

Intercourse in marriage is a means of giving love and pleasure to the other, but even more, it is a way of receiving what the other is able to give. The mark of love is being able to accept what the other person is able and willing to give at that moment and, beyond accepting it, delighting in it. This goes beyond rules.

Someone recently described the Arab-Israeli war as a tragedy because both sides are right. In marriage, when we read a book to discover what positions for intercourse are permissible, or what the other person ought to find permissible, we have already created a tragedy where both sides are right and, therefore, both sides are wrong. Practically speaking, if I want to improve our sex life, I would get better results by buying *The Sensuous Man* for myself than by buying *The Sensuous Woman* for my wife.

4. *What about the frequency of intercourse in marriage?* Just as there is no right position, there is no average frequency. When one begins to ask this ques-

tion, one is really trying to find out where his or her mate is failing, either in demanding too much or in not giving enough. There will always be an inequality of appetite, and this in itself is part of the whole communication game in marriage. God ought to make it possible for us to enjoy being on either side of this continuing dialogue. Often the name of the game is actually power and not sex. It is illuminating to find that when one partner adopts the more passive sex role in a marriage the other invariably becomes the aggressor. In other words, the role of the demanding one or the passive one is more a psychological power play than the result of a physical sex drive.

5. *What about extramarital sex?* The Bible is very clear about this and speaks often and strongly against adultery. One of the original Ten Commandments is a flat "Thou shalt not commit adultery." I mentioned the reasons for this earlier. Adultery is wrong because intercourse is a means of mystical union which makes two people one. Adultery is always harmful and against God's best plan for man. But I feel we have blown it up out of all proportion until it has become "the unforgivable sin." We feel much less strongly about coveting or not honoring your father and mother, for example. This commandment must be seen in proportion with the other nine. It's strange how we seldom hear of a Christian wife divorcing her husband because he doesn't honor his father and mother or covets his boss's job.

6. *What about divorce?* The Bible seems clear that divorce is wrong. But so is war, yet sometimes that is the lesser of two evils. What happens when two people find that even though they are both Christians, they cannot live together creatively? It may be that divorce is a way out for both. To stay married for the sake of

the children does irreparable harm to the children and there is no justification for that. To stay married in order to fulfill some law of God that destroys people is no law of God. And even though it is not what God planned for man, it may be better than staying married to someone you wish were dead, for that is murder, or imagining that you are married to someone else, for that is adultery.

The real issue here is to help a person understand what real love and responsibility would look like for him and the others involved.

7. *What about pornography?* To read a pornographic book, if you're a salesman in a strange motel room or a lonely widow on a cold night, is dumb. It's like standing in front of a bakery window, broke and hungry. To read pornography when there is no legitimate means of fulfilling your sex drive is dumb. To read pornography when you already have so much sex drive you can't handle it is dumb. But if you are the passive partner in a marriage, it seems to me that reading of erotic literature is not only justifiable but even desirable. This is not a case for pornography but a case for finding ways to undo some of the psychological damage done to many of us years ago so that our marriage can be more fulfilling for our partner.

8. *What about the single person?* The Bible certainly seems to commend the single state to many though it warns that no one should try to live this way by sheer will power unless there is a predisposition of some kind or a special gift of God's grace in this area. In the Roman Catholic tradition it seems that the single life is better than the married life. In the Protestant tradition we have implied that the married life is better than the single life. I think both views are nonsense. Jesus Christ came to make us whole people.

It is our personhood that he is concerned about, more than our married or single state.

The loneliness of the single person is no more or less painful than the loneliness of many married people. In counseling a single person the important thing is to help that person understand why he or she is single. This can prove liberating. Many singles have asked me what I think about sex for single people. I think the real question is, "What does your singleness say about you?"

Some people are single because they have set goals that are much too high. They are looking for a Mr. or Miss Right who will never come along. He or she is a combination of Daddy, Johnny Carson, Tarzan, and Norman Vincent Peale. That person just does not exist. The person is single because he or she has never accepted his or her own humanity and the humanity of others.

On the other hand, there are people who are single because of a great fear of rejection. I just spent a number of days at a conference with a lovely single girl. At one point she could finally tell all of us that her singlensss came out of this fear of being rejected. She often became emotionally involved with married men because they were simply off-limits. To compete for single men her own age so terrified her that she retreated, loudly proclaiming to all that she loved her freedom as a single person. This young woman is now moving into a new dimension in understanding her own personhood and her own goals.

Some people are single because of their low self-esteem. They cannot believe that anybody could love them. I have known some really attractive men and women who did not date because they could not imagine anybody caring to become involved with them emotionally, let alone romantically.

To assume that people are single because of happenstance in this day and age is naïve. Most single people have some other problem at work in their life. We need to help them see this and give them the support and acceptance they need to move out into freedom.

Finally, there are single people who have weighed both sides and prefer their freedom to the companionship married life offers. These people have been penalized in our society. I've heard one friend lament that dinner parties can never be held for an odd number of people. She is invariably asked to come and bring a man. This says to her that she is unacceptable alone. Just as the Roman Catholic tradition has made second-class citizens of married people, so our Western Protestant tradition has made second-class citizens of single people. Let's affirm that God is for people, single or married!

9. *What about the homosexual?* I've already suggested that part of the problem of the homosexual will be solved when we stop assigning male and female roles to people. We need to understand that in the area of homosexuality our job is not to condemn the homosexual but to love him, have concern for him, and help him whenever possible to enter into some kind of heterosexual life where there is a hope for fulfillment. I do not know a single homosexual who is happy to be what he is. On the surface they say, "Gay is great," but underneath it's a long, tired, hard, lonely road. There are many people caught in the homosexual trap who would not be there if they could have a friend who would believe in them and for them and help them accept their role but not their state.

10. *What about masturbation?* I think we've come a long way from the old days when it was thought that masturbation was mentally and physically harmful.

Charlie Shedd, in his wonderful, whimsical book, *The Stork Is Dead,* has a chapter entitled "Masturbation: God's Gift to the Teenager." This has really disturbed a number of people who cannot adjust to thinking of this old taboo as a gift. Certainly masturbation can be the way God has given for easing what seems like intolerable tension, both for the single and the married. But I don't know of anyone who practices masturbation from time to time who does not feel guilty afterwards. The happy Portnoy does not seem to exist.

Basically, it seems to me that masturbation is a way of literally taking your destiny in your own hands. For the Christian to masturbate, single or married, puts him in the place where he says to God, "I can run my own life. I no longer trust you to provide for my sexuality. I'll do it for myself." Masturbation is not bad, but it is certainly not God's best. To refrain from it can be a new way of trusting him.

*11. What is the biblical view of sex?* I can find nothing in the Bible that implies that sex is evil. On the contrary, I find evidence that sex is good, that intercourse is good, and that marriage is good. In Genesis 1:27 we find "God created man in his own image, . . . male and female created he them." In Genesis 1:31 we find "God saw everything that he had made, and, behold, it was very good."

Even beyond that, the New Testament talks about the new fellowship called the church or the Body of Christ. And it is described in terms of a marriage, with Christ the bridegroom and us believers as the bride. Marriage and the marriage bed seem to be honored over and over again in Scripture and, indeed, used as an illustration for the most intimate relationship between Christ and his people.

Finally, we have this injunction from Paul, "To the

pure all things are pure, but to the corrupt and un-believing nothing is pure" (Tit. 1:15, RSV).

One last word. The week before I wrote this chap-ter, I led a workshop on marriage in Topeka, Kansas. I asked each person in the group to write what he or she would like to hang in the home of every married couple in the world if they could. Here are a few: "Fight fair." "Don't give up." "Keep on keeping on." "Pray for patience." "No peace at any price." "Enjoy the journey."

For a Christian to be married is not easy. For a Christian to be single has many problems. Whatever our state, let's learn how to celebrate God's gift of sexuality in responsible ways.

# 9

# Ask Me to Dance

The church is full of people of faith asking us to teach them to dance. They remind me of the people in the crowd, standing steadfast and faithful but somehow unable to join King David as he dances with joyful abandon before the ark of the Lord God. In the background hovers David's wife, Michal, herself the daughter of King Saul. Of royal blood and trying desperately to do the proper thing, she shouts stage instructions to her husband, "Come in, you're making a fool of yourself. After all, you're the king! Quit it!" She sounds very much like a suburban housewife at a neighborhood party where her husband has put a lampshade on his head or is doing his bird calls.

In the crowd surrounding David are people who by any humanly measurable degree are less sinful than their king. They had trusted God; they had even confessed their sins and been forgiven, but they are not dancing. Like Lazarus who came forth from the tomb filled with life but bound by graveclothes, they are unable to leap or sing or to experience the exhilaration and freedom that David expresses.

Just as in the church of the Old Testament, the church of the new covenant, now two thousand years old, is full of people who are alive by the grace of God, who trust and believe in him, and who are asking to dance. They are intrigued by an authentic person like David, released to live life to the full, or like Martin Luther, who seemed to live with joy and abandon in spite of making many mistakes. This is what the cure of souls is all about.

I know all Greeks are not like Zorba, but they are a happy people who know how to dance. A group of Greek Christians touring Britain had an interesting reaction to the Church of England services they attended at Coventry Cathedral.

In our country, we come to church feeling happy. We greet our friends and we go inside to worship with a sense of freedom. Here, you march up to the church looking grim and greeting no one. You behave inside like soldiers on parade, sitting in rows with your eyes to the front, all getting up and sitting down together at the word of command from your superior officer.

In reacting to this description of him and his church, Steven Verney says:

Of course, this is partly due to our national temperament, for we like things to be done decently and in order, but my Greek friends are not altogether wrong in laughing at our stiffness, for worship ought to be the moment at which we are most natural and completely ourselves. If we take ourselves very seriously, and are afraid to stand up, sit down, sing too loud, or join the responses lest we make ourselves conspicuous, then we must be making it very difficult indeed for the Holy Spirit to inspire our prayers. It is all too common for a church service to be so tense and unnatural that when the worshippers get home, they explode in quarrels with one another, and the effect of this rigidity is particularly devastating to children. Seeing their parents afraid even to smile when something funny happens, they find it difficult to believe that they are really in the house of a Father who loves them.[1]

In America as well, churches have been filled with these solid, faithful, gray people who never do anything very wrong but who have never experienced the hope in Jesus Christ that enables them to dance in and through life. These people are our church's greatest potential. In its most relevant moments, the church has had a concern for people who have serious moral, mental, or physical problems. But the vast bulk of people who fill pews, staff committees, and pay costs are overlooked. These are the people of faith who are saying, "Ask me to dance."

Let us hope that these days of churchly dullness and sanctimonious rigidity are in their death throes. Several years ago in Tremont Temple, a gifted Methodist preacher told a thousand of his fellow preachers, "You know, worship today bores me. It even bores me when I am preaching!" This same friend has begun an experimental church in his own neighborhood in Atlanta. Across the country innovative Christians are discovering that in addition to worship, people can find and give help to one another in the name of Christ. The dance of joy becomes authentic posture for released people, living in wholeness with meaning.

This newly emerging church will be marked by a new kind of clinical syncretism. In the decades past the church has attempted some kind of theological syncretism, or doctrinal syncretism. In other words, there has been an effort to bring together all the basic strands of belief and faith into one central church. The Council of Churches and the attempt at church mergers have been built on the hope that we could find theological agreement. This may always elude us, and we may have to settle for varied shades of conviction and belief within the church. But we can have a clinical syncretism where we agree on those things that make for life, be they secular or sacred, and bring them into the service of Christ and his church.

We have been discussing six dimensions in which God can bring wholeness for a person. You may know of any number of places that are focusing on one piece of this pie of wholeness and doing a fantastic job. What I am suggesting is that the church begin to put these components together and make them available as a package for all those seeking help and growth and release.

The volitional, with which we began, emphasizes the tremendous importance of the will in the cure of souls. For hundreds of years pietists and evangelicals have made much of this, and we can learn from them the importance of making an opportunity available for this decision of the will. Part of the success of a Billy Graham crusade, for instance, must be in the fact that it is one of the few settings that provide such an opportunity in our day.

The convictions we hold shape our motivation and our conduct. The liberal part of the church, both Roman and Protestant, has for centuries specialized in this conceptual dimension of life—educating the minds and elevating the thoughts of men.

Through the confessional dimension, God provides a way for us to have our real guilt dealt with and forgiven. For two thousand years the Roman Catholic church has stressed the necessity and the therapeutic value of confession. In more recent times, as Protestantism rejected the value of confession, mental illness has grown and modern psychiatry, under its father Freud, has thrived. But the Freudians, as well as the

Roman Catholics, have taught us much about the dynamics and therapy of confession.

The area of the emotional is a more recent area of interest and concern for people wishing to help their fellow-men. Today the behavioral sciences and the fast-growing human potential movement are doing tremendous research and experimentation to release emotions in people that they might live fuller lives. From places like Esalen and its hundreds of counterparts all across the country, including the National Training Labs, we can discover methods to harness and use in the cure of souls within the structure of the church.

The fifth piece of our pie is the relational dimension. Very simply put, the things that we do and say and are with the significant people in our lives affect us and affect them and make for wholeness. The transactional analysis school of psychiatry, led by men such as Harris, Glasser, Jourard, Berne, Mowrer and others, has given us tremendous insights about how we can help people to live beyond the feeling level in responsible everyday behavior.

Finally, we examined the physical dimension of life, on the thesis that the body is not a house in which people live but a part and parcel of the mind and soul. Of course, the whole psychosomatic school of medicine has been flourishing for more than thirty years. Recently, others have been doing research in the area of body language. This is a tremendously fertile field for study here as we consider our total ministry to people.

As the Gospel records Jesus encountering individuals, we see him practicing the cure of souls. Seldom does he say the same thing to two different people. To one person he gives a physical command,

"Take up your bed and walk." To another he gives a deeply spiritual command, "You must be born again." To a person with an emotional or mental problem and a very real identity crisis, he says, "What is your name?" To another Jesus says, "Be cleansed," while to the man who has a problem with possessions, he says, "Sell all that you have and give it to the poor." It is amazing how we have universalized Jesus' command about being born again, but we say very little of Jesus' diagnosis for the rich young ruler, "Sell all that you have and give it to the poor." I am suggesting that we practice this Jesus ministry with one another. It seems so simple; yet apart from the Holy Spirit using one person to help another, it is impossible.

Myron Madden, author of the book *The Power to Bless,* is one of the most gifted counselors I know. I asked Myron one day about his method of counseling and he replied very simply, "I ask people what it is they really want in life and what they have to give up to attain that." Such a simple yet profound approach can help each of us to become an effective counselor.

Many of us have prayed for a long time for God to send his Spirit to explode the church and save the world, but maybe the best way to save the world is for the church to implode. It's very much like the pumpkin that we put in our backyard after Halloween. After several months the pumpkin still looked in wonderful shape until one day it imploded. It simply caved in. Maybe this is the new kind of Pentecost needed. If there were an implosion, there might later be an explosion that could truly shake the world.

One church, Broadway Baptist in Kansas City, has dared to believe that the church's primary function is not mission but fellowship. It believes that Christ called into being, by the power of the Holy Spirit, a fellowship of people who could learn to care deeply for one another. This church does exactly that. The pastor visits with no more than twelve to eighteen people each week. (They are the same twelve to eighteen people each week!) These people in turn begin to care for others in groups of twelve to eighteen, who in turn care for others. The pastor makes almost no house calls or hospital calls but leaves the ministry of caring for one another to members of his church. They are not only reaching out and touching the lives of many people on the outside, they are discovering a new kind of life and caring on the inside.

Richard Wurmbrand, a Protestant minister who spent fourteen years in a Communist prison in Rumania, tells this story. He once asked a boy if he believed in the divinity of Christ. The boy answered no. His reason: "If Jesus is God, He should be able to do the things that God does. God made roses and roses make other roses. God made elephants and elephants make other elephants. If Jesus is God, He should be able to do the things that God does. He should be able to make other Jesuses. But I have never seen one. My mother takes in washing and has no time for me. My father is an alcoholic. Nobody was ever kind to me, so I never met Jesus." Wurmbrand said he asked the boy then, "But isn't your pastor another Jesus?" "No!" came the emphatic reply. When Wurmbrand later told the pastor what the youth had said, the pastor answered, "That crazy kid."

George Bernard Shaw's play *Heartbreak House* was performed as a revival on Broadway recently. I tore out and saved the review by Walter Kerr because it so captured our situation in the church:

As planes roar, bombs fall and the mast of the ship of States sways wildly in the third act of Heartbreak House. It is perfectly clear what George Bernard Shaw is trying to tell us. He is saying that although the modern world is peopled with some of the nicest, most attractive, most outspoken, most intelligent, most forgiving folk God ever created, the rudderless vessel in which they are all complacently drifting, is going to split on the rocks and sink. The trouble is that our prophetic playwright made his drifting figures so nice, so attractive, so outspoken, so intelligent and so forgiving that the warning isn't worth a fig. Come off it, we say. They're a lovely lot and they needn't be bothered about bombs now.[2]

We must cease to be so nice and begin to be real. We need to become aware of one another. We need to discover that people are like us, that people hurt in the ways that we hurt and that we can be God's answer to one another within the fellowship of the church.

This kind of caring for people not only marks the level of life within the fellowship, but it marks the relationship that the people of God have with those outside of the church. In its simplest terms this is evangelism. People on the outside need to know that people on the inside care about them, not just about their pledge or their initial commitment but about the whole shape of their life. Even more elementary, people outside need to know that people inside are genuinely glad to see them.

Some time ago I received a letter from a businessman in Pittsburgh who tried to visit us at our Faith at Work office when it was located in New York City. Apparently, he misread the address and came to a very different place. Listen to his letter:

Dear Bruce,

Sorry to miss you when I was in New York last week. Guess you fellows are hip deep planning for a conference at this time. Would be wonderful to be with you. In the last issue of Faith at Work Magazine, you indicated that your staff would welcome us "with open arms." I took you at your word and proceeded to what I thought was your address . . . Wow, it seemed like a strange place for the Faith at Work office, but then, I thought, these are peculiar people. It was an old office building with a large blood bank on the second floor. I figured you must be on the third floor, so I entered the open door into the hallway to look at the mailboxes. As I did, a buxom woman came into full view and with coaxing voice, said, "Come on up, doll boy, we're waiting for you.". . . [he goes on to say] . . . Now Bruce, as much as I appreciate your desire to make us visitors to New York welcome, I do think that's carrying this "open arms" bit a little far! By the way, next time I'll get your address straight and come to your real office.

We have laughed about that letter, but I have often thought the warmth of the welcome he describes is the very warmth the church ought to be able to convey to people on the outside. "We are glad to see you, we've been waiting for you, come on in, how have you been?"

Central Lutheran Church in downtown Minneapolis has been trying to do just that. A couple of years ago they decided to do something about self-preservation. Listen to what the pastor, Orin Thompson, says: "We were an edifice of size and cold grey stone sprinkled with stained glass. None of the people in this neighborhood felt they could come in. When we decided that all we had was Christ's love, we decided that we had to give it away or give it up. . . . We did this through modern communications which created a feeling of hope in this neighborhood. They came to us and we reached out to them in a way that we never thought possible."[3] This is the church, incidentally, that put signs on the sides of buses all over Minneapolis, saying, "I love you. Is that O.K.? /s/ Jesus C."

All of this comes from taking people seriously. This kind of ministry is not generated artificially. Rather, it is a natural outpouring of simply being who you are and caring for other people and caring how they are.

I remember reading about a black girl who moved here from Angola in West Africa. Her name was Maria and she was always laughing. One day she went to a meeting on evangelism in her church where they were talking about pamphlets, missions, campaigns, and all the rest. At one point someone turned to Maria and said, "What do they do in your church in Angola, Maria?" "In my church," said Maria, after a moment's thought, "we don't give pamphlets to people or have missions. We just send one or two Christian families to live in a village. And when people see what Christians are like, then they want to be Christians themselves."[4] It seems to me that this simplicity and artlessness is the key to evangelism in the church.

Dr. Henry Van Dusen opened new doors to me in his book *Spirit, Son and Father* when he described this style in theological terms. He says that the New Testament benediction was simply "Spirit, Son and Father" but we have reversed this in our day and say instead, "In the name of the Father, Son and Holy Spirit." This is because we have reversed the New Testament strategy in approaching people. We come to people first of all with the doctrine of God the Father, which is the most difficult of the Christian doctrines to comprehend. We then talk about the doctrine of the Son, which is more understandable, and finally, we save the Holy Spirit for those inside the church who are most mature. Van Dusen says this is wrong, that we should begin with the Holy Spirit himself. The outsider can understand the Spirit of God loose in people, even as in the people of Central Church in Minneapolis. As people respond to the warmth of the Spirit in other people, they can then be taught about the Son, and finally, as they mature, grapple with the doctrine of God the Father.

We are hearing from the secular world a prediction that new leadership will come, not from charismatic leaders, but from the grassroots. Saul Alinsky and John Gardner alike are saying that the only hope for America to become a new society is to produce ordinary, everyday people at the grassroots who will take responsibility for their little part of the city, town, kingdom, church, school, wherever they are.

This is what the New Testament brought into being, and we are rediscovering it today. Each believer has in his power the ability to release the potential for healing and wholeness in others. We can be liberators. We are those to whom Jesus turns and says, "Loose him and let him go."

We have given tremendous lip service to the doctrine of the priesthood of all belevers, but we have been slow to practice it. The comic strip "B.C." recently described our situation. B.C., sitting in his fur loincloth, opens a box. The letter in the box says, "Congratulations! You have just purchased the world's finest fire-starting kit!" The next picture shows him reading on, "The flint is of the finest stone imported from the Orient. Your striker has been handcrafted by Old World craftsmen. The kindling has been carefully selected by screened lumberjacks. Your kit was packaged and inspected by little old grannies working in a dust-free environment, and your fire kit dealer has sworn an oath of devotion to customers." In the next picture B.C. is rubbing two sticks together. When one of the cavewomen comes by and says, "What's with the sticks? Where is your new fire-starting kit?" he looks up, smiles and says, "I built a shrine around it."

Have we in the church taken all the wonderful equipment God has given us and turned it into a useless shrine? It is time that we used the equipment for ministry that God has so lavishly and generously given us and practiced the cure of souls in the church. Each of us must begin to be responsible for a few other people in a way that can bring radical changes. Let's take them by the hand, listen to them, believe in them, believe for them. Let's help them discover the part of their life that hurts the most, that needs healing the most, that is most ready to respond. It is time that we heard people around us saying, "Ask me to dance."

# QUESTIONS FOR REFLECTION
## OR DISCUSSION

### CHAPTER I

1. Rethink your own biography, spiritual or otherwise. What are the radical changes that God has made in your life? What changes do you think are still ahead of you?

2. Can you identify with Lazarus? Has any part of his experience been yours? If so, when and where?

3. Have you ever had the experience of ministering to another and helping him to discover new freedom and new life?

4. Remembering the Church of the Holy Achievers and the Church of Dynamic Doormatism, list the message, strengths, and weaknesses of your church. If you were to start a church, what would it be like?

5. How do you react to the quote by Carl Jung? How far have you come in loving yourself? Who has helped you to do this? Have you ever helped another to love himself?

### CHAPTER II

1. If you have ever thought of the specific cost involved in turning your life over to Jesus Christ,

whether you made the decision or not, describe what you understood to be this cost.

2. If you have made this decision, describe the help you received from other person(s).

3. If you have ever helped another to take this step of commitment, describe what you did and what happened to the person.

4. What would you say to someone who sees no need for a commitment to Jesus Christ?

5. How would you help the person who is committed to Jesus Christ but who is indifferent to the world's needs?

6. Have you ever made a covenant with several other people or a large group? Did you keep it? How did it work? What was involved in the covenant?

7. If you were going to make a covenant with some other people, what would you like to see as part of it and how would it work?

8. Has your commitment to the person of Christ helped you to understand the problem of your own identity?

CHAPTER III

1. Outside of the Bible, what three books have been most influential in your own understanding of Christian philosophy or the landscape of reality? How would you paraphrase the key thought in each of those books in two or three sentences each?

2. If you could write a book, produce a movie, or direct a television show, what is the central message that you would like to communicate to the greatest number of people?

3. Complete in one sentence each of the four following phrases:

    a. My reason for living is _____

    b. My reason for dying is _____

    c. My understanding of evil is _____

    d. My strategy for the promotion and increase of righteousness is _____

4. Who is the greatest teacher that you have ever known? What did he or she say or do that made him or her so effective in your life?

### CHAPTER IV

1. Do you think there is a connection between being able to be wrong and staying young?

2. If you have ever considered opening your life totally to another person as an act of spiritual discipline, describe your feelings and your fears at that time.

3. Who has been the Ananias in your life? What did he or she do and/or say? What was his relationship to you? What was your response? What changes have come in your life?

4. To whom have you been an Ananias? What was the opportunity? What was the cost to you? How did you follow through? What changes could you see God bringing about in the life of the other?

### CHAPTER V

1. Have you ever had the experience of being thoroughly turned off by somebody who believes in all the same things in which you believe? Analyze why you were turned off.

2. Have you ever come to appreciate and enjoy, and even like, someone whose values and goals are very different from your own? What was there about

this person that drew you into a deep caring, enjoyable relationship?

3. At this moment, think of the most meaningful relationship in your life. Ask yourself why this relationship is so meaningful. What is this other person being or doing and how are you responding that is allowing God to make this relationship a source of help for you and the other person? What can you learn from this relationship about what God is trying to do in the area of the relational?

4. At this moment, what is the most frustrating relationship in your life? Think of what you are doing or not doing with this other person that is inhibiting the relationship from being real, creative, or loving. What do you think God is trying to teach you in this relationship?

CHAPTER VI

1. Which emotion do you have the greatest difficulty expressing or controlling?

2. Trace the relationships and events in your early life that have made you the way you are emotionally.

3. How would you describe the way you personally handle emotions? Are you free and expressive? Or are you inhibited and guarded? Do you allow others to express their emotions? Or do you inhibit them?

4. What changes would you like to see in the way you handle feelings? What do you think would be the cost to you of having to change?

5. Have you ever helped someone else who was having difficulty handling his negative feelings? What did you do or what could you have done to help set him free?

CHAPTER VII

1. What do you think your body says to people? Look at your total impression, including facial expressions, posture, attitude, eyes and mouth especially. Do you think that your body says to strangers and friends the thing you want it to say? Does it say the thing that is really true about you?

2. Think of a close friend or family member. What do you think his or her body says about him or her? See how closely you can read the signs if it is true that your body does not lie.

3. Think of the weakest link in your physical make-up. What can you learn from the area of your chronic illness?

4. Have a dialogue with that particular part of your body or organ. Talk to it and then act the part of the body and talk back to yourself. See if you can learn what it is trying to tell you and how you can cooperate with it.

CHAPTER VIII

1. What do you understand to be your greatest need at the moment in the area of the sexual? Have you found a creative way to handle that need? What does that need say about your general needs at this time: your need for power, your confusion about identity, your goals, the relational dimensions of your life, and so on?

2. What is your attitude toward sex? Do you think it is healthy, unhealthy, or inhibited? What were the early influences in your life that gave you your attitude?

3. Are you the kind of person to whom others speak about their sexual needs, longings, desires? If not, analyze why not. If so, describe how you help others to understand what is happening in the sexual dimension of life.

CHAPTER IX

Questions to ask another as you are trying to practice the cure of souls:

1. Who is now running your life? On what basis do you make decisions?

2. What is your strategy for making the world and people happier and better?

3. Do you have any secrets or hidden places in your life that have not been shared with another person?

4. How do you handle your negative feelings? In a creative way or a destructive way?

5. Are you basically a Jesus or a John the Baptist in your relationships with others? Do you point out their faults and criticize them or do you affirm them and believe in them as they are?

6. What do you think your body is telling you about who you are and what your needs are right now?

7. If your sexual life is a barometer of where you are, what do you think it is saying to you right now about your own needs and goals?

8. Since it's never too late to change, why don't we pray and ask God for help.

# SELECTED BIBLIOGRAPHY

CHAPTER II

There are a great many excellent books for resource in this dimension. Many classics, of course, and then some of the popular contemporary books by men such as Billy Graham, Brian Green, and John Stott.

Ford, Leighton. *The Christian Persuader*. New York: Harper & Row, 1966.

James, William. *Varieties of Religious Experience*. New York: Macmillan, 1961.

Jones, E. Stanley. *Conversion*. Nashville: Abingdon, 1959.

Larson, Bruce. *Dare to Live Now*. Grand Rapids, Mich.: Zondervan, 1967.

Lewis, C. S. *Mere Christianity*. New York: Macmillan, 1952.

Marshall, Catherine. *Beyond Ourselves*. Old Tappan, N.J.: Revell, 1968.

Miller, Keith. *Taste of New Wine*. Waco, Texas: Word Books, 1965.

O'Connor, Elizabeth. *Call to Commitment*. New York: Harper & Row, 1963.

Shoemaker, Samuel. *How to Become a Christian*. New York: Harper & Row, 1953.

Trueblood, Elton. *The Company of the Committed*. New York: Harper & Row, 1961.

CHAPTER III

There is such a wealth for the serious student that one hardly knows where to begin. Great and helpful thinkers cover every shade of the Christian spectrum. I have personally been much influenced by men like Karl Barth, Emil Brunner, Reinhold Niebuhr, and Paul Tillich. In a more contemporary, evangelical vein there are the many books by Francis Schaeffer that are most helpful.

Barth, Karl. *Epistle to the Romans*. Translated by Edwyn C. Hoskyns. 6th ed. New York: Oxford University Press, 1968.

Brunner, Emil. *The Misunderstanding of the Church*. Philadelphia: Westminster, 1953.

Chambers, Whittaker. *Witness*. New York: Random House, 1952.

Larson, Bruce, and Osborne, Ralph. *The Emerging Church*. Waco, Texas: Word Books, 1970.

Latourette, Kenneth Scott. *History of the Expansion of Christianity*. 7 vols. New York: Harper & Bros., 1945.

Lewis, C. S. *The Lion, the Witch and the Wardrobe*. New York: Macmillan, 1951.

————. *Out of the Silent Planet*. New York: Macmillan, 1965.

————. *Perelandra*. New York: Macmillan, 1944.

————. *That Hideous Strength*. New York: Macmillan, 1968.

Niebuhr, Reinhold. *The Nature and Destiny of Man.* New York: Scribner's, 1949.

O'Connor, Elizabeth. *Journey Inward, Journey Outward.* New York: Harper & Row, 1968.

Stringfellow, William. *My People Is the Enemy.* New York: Holt, Rinehart, and Winston, 1964.

Van Dusen, Henry P. *Spirit, Son and Father.*

## CHAPTER IV

There is a great deal of helpful material in this dimension in the writings of the founding fathers of psychoanalysis, including Sigmund Freud, Carl Jung, and Felix Adler. There is also a wealth of books in the Roman Catholic tradition about the history of confession in the church.

Grubb, Norman. *Continuous Revival.* Fort Washington, Pa.: Christian Literature Crusade, 1961.

Hession, Roy. *The Calvary Road.* Fort Washington, Pa.: Christian Literature Crusade, 1964.

Jourard, Sidney. *The Transparent Self.* New York: Van Nostrand-Reinhold, 1964.

Larson, Bruce. *No Longer Strangers.* Waco, Texas: Word Books, 1971.

Milliken, Bill, and Meredith, Charles. *Tough Love.* Old Tappan, N.J.: Revell, 1968.

Mowrer, Hobart. *The Crisis in Psychiatry and Religion.* New York: Van Nostrand-Reinhold, 1961.

———. *The New Group Therapy.* New York: Van Nostrand-Reinhold, 1964.

Tournier, Paul. *The Meaning of Persons.* New York: Harper & Row, 1957.

Weatherhead, Leslie. *Psychology, Religion and Healing.* Nashville: Abingdon.

CHAPTER V

In addition to the books listed here, see especially the writings of Lyman Coleman.

Berne, Eric. *Games People Play*. New York: Grove Press, 1964.

Glasser, William. *Reality Therapy*. New York: Harper & Row, 1965.

Harris, Thomas. *I'm O.K.; You're O.K.* New York: Harper & Row, 1969.

Larson, Bruce. *No Longer Strangers*. Waco, Texas: Word Books, 1971.

———. *Living on the Growing Edge*. Grand Rapids, Mich.: Zondervan, 1968.

———. *Setting Men Free*. Grand Rapids, Mich.; Zondervan, 1967.

Miller, Keith. *A Second Touch*. Waco, Texas: Word Books, 1967.

Milliken, Bill, and Meredith, Charles. *Tough Love*. Old Tappan, N.J.: Revell, 1968.

Ogilvie, Lloyd. *A Life Full of Surprises*. Nashville: Abingdon, 1969.

Shedd, Charlie. *Letters to Karen*. Nashville: Abingdon, 1965.

———. *Promises to Peter*. Waco, Texas: Word Books, 1970.

Stephens, Overton. *Today Is All You Have*.

Whiston, Lionel A. *Are You Fun to Live With?* Waco, Texas: Word Books, 1968.

CHAPTER VI

Howard, Jane. *Please Touch*. New York: McGraw-Hill, 1970.

Laing, R. D. *The Divided Self*. New York: Barnes & Noble, 1960.

———. *Knots*. New York: Random House (Pantheon), 1970.

———. *The Self and Others*. New York: Random House (Pantheon), 1970.

Miller, Keith. *Habitation of Dragons*. Waco, Texas: Word Books, 1970.

Schutz, William. *Here Comes Everybody*.

———. *Joy*. New York: Grove Press, 1967.

CHAPTER VII

There is a great deal of early research done thirty or more years ago by men such as Franz Alexander and Flanders Dunbar in the area of psychosomatic medicine. More recently, men such as Karl Menninger and Paul Tournier have written marvelous helpful books that touch on the area of the physical.

Fast, Julius. *Body Language*. Philadelphia: M. Evans, 1970.

McMillen, S. I. *None of These Diseases*. Old Tappan, N.J.: Revell, 1963.

May, Rollo. *Love and Will*. New York: W. W. Norton, 1969.

Schindler, John. *How to Live 365 Days a Year*. New York: Prentice-Hall, 1954.

CHAPTER VIII

The variety of books available in this area is limitless and defies any kind of classification or description. Some are wonderfully helpful and some are questionable or harmful. I am listing two of the most recent books simply because they are fresh and helpful.

Reuben, David. *Everything You Always Wanted to Know about Sex . . . But Were Afraid to Ask.* New York: David McKay, 1969.

Shedd, Charlie. *The Stork Is Dead.* Waco, Texas: Word Books, 1968.

# NOTES

INTRODUCTION

1. R. D. Laing, *Knots* (New York: Pantheon Books, 1970), p. 1.
2. Wes Seeliger, *Faith at Work*, February 1972, p. 13.

CHAPTER I

1. Lee Maxwell, "God Exhales."
2. Carl Jung, *Psychological Reflections*, ed. Jolande Jacobi (Princeton, N.J.: Princeton University Press, 1970).

CHAPTER II

1. William James, *Varieties of Religious Experience* (London: Longmans Green and Co., 1902).
2. Dorothy Parker, "The Veteran," *The Portable Dorothy Parker* (New York: Viking Press, 1954).
3. Dietrich Bonhoeffer, *Letters and Papers from Prison*, rev. ed., ed. Eberhard Bethge (New York: Macmillan, 1967), pp. 188–89.

CHAPTER III

1. Whittaker Chambers, *Witness* (New York: Random House, 1952).
2. Ibid.

CHAPTER IV

1. Sidney M. Jourard, *The Transparent Self* (New York: Van Nostrand-Reinhold, 1971).

CHAPTER V

1. Paul Tournier, *The Meaning of Persons* (New York: Harper & Row, 1957).
2. Margery Williams, *The Velveteen Rabbit* (New York: Doubleday, 1958), p. 17.

CHAPTER VI

1. "The Mental Health of Presbyterian Ministers and Their Families," Presbyterian Church in the U.S., Atlanta, Georgia.
2. Peter DeVries, *Into Your Tent I'll Creep* (Boston: Little, Brown & Co., 1971), p. 38.

CHAPTER VII

1. Henry Robinson, "Skin Patient Work Held Encouraging," *Baltimore Sun*, 8 December 1971.
2. Quoted in Jane Howard, *Please Touch* (New York: Dell Publications, 1970), p. 30.
3. Quoted in ibid., p. 32.

CHAPTER IX

1. Steven Verney, *Fire in Coventry* (Westwood, N.J.: Fleming H. Revell, 1965).

2. Walter Kerr, review of George Bernard Shaw, "Heartbreak House," *New York Herald Tribune*, 19 October 1959.

3. Ron Bacigalupo, "Love Is Where It's At in the Core City," *Twin Citian Magazine*, December 1970.

4. Verney, *Fire in Coventry*.